From Regulatory Policies to International Arbitration

Mehmet Nar

From Regulatory Policies to International Arbitration

Political Economy

PETER LANG

Bibliographic Information published by the Deutsche Nationalbibliothek
The Deutsche Nationalbibliothek lists this publication in the Deutsche Nationalbibliografie; detailed bibliographic data is available online at http://dnb.d-nb.de.

Library of Congress Cataloging-in-Publication Data
A CIP catalog record for this book has been applied for at the Library of Congress.

ISBN 978-3-631-89067-7 (Print)
E-ISBN 978-3-631-89128-5 (E-PDF)
E-ISBN 978-3-631-89129-2 (E-PUB)
10.3726/b20253

Peter Lang – Berlin · Bruxelles · Lausanne · New York · Oxford

This publication has been peer reviewed.

www.peterlang.com

Prof. Dr. Mehmet Şükrü NAR
Esra NAR
and to Yiğit Alp NAR

Preface

Today, it is not possible to understand economic problems and make realistic analyses without focusing on political policies. Therefore, it is necessary to try to fully understand the relations between economic science and political science. This book focuses on the basic concepts of political economy. Fundamental issues of national and international political economy and exemplary problems encountered in practice are evaluated. The whole of relations arising from economic science, political science, and power relations is taken up with an interdisciplinary approach.

The differences between the two fields of science are actually due to an artificial divergence. However, there are always favorable conditions that reveal the unity between economics and political science. In particular, the attempt to gain benefits, which shows the effect of politics on the markets, constitutes a clear example of this unity. Many forms of economic thought – from the Virginia School of Political Economy to public choice analysis, from constitutional economic theory to institutional economics – draw attention to the impact of politics on the economy and the contribution of this process to individual interest.

This study explains how the government itself, which is seen as a mechanism for resource allocation and efficiency in the market, can cause inefficiency. It evaluates how the whole of the relations between two defective structures – the market and the government – can actually work for the benefit of some but to the detriment of the society, and how this bundle of relations is reflected on the national and international political economy.

This work is an original study in which interdependent variables are analyzed together. After the theoretical framework, explanatory information on political economy and international politics is shared with the reader, accompanied by up-to-date data. Unlike in similar books on political economy, here problems are evaluated with short and simple explanations. This first edition of the book is an original work, and will be a useful resource for all researchers and social scientists interested in the subject. I hope it will be useful to those who are interested.

Prof. Dr. Mehmet NAR

Ankara-Turkey
Thursday, June 23, 2022

Contents

List of Figures

List of Tables

List of Graphs

List of Abbreviations

AAA:	American Arbitration Association
ADR :	Alternative Dispute Resolution
AMPPI:	Agreement on the Mutual Protection and Promotion of Investments
APA :	Advance pricing arrangement
BAP:	Binding Arbitration Procedure
CCC:	Commodity Credit Corporation
CCT:	Common Customs Tariff
CFTC:	Commodity Futures Trading Commission
CIETAC:	China International Economic and Trade Arbitration Commission
COVID-19:	Coronavirus Disease
CT:	Capture Theory
DTAA:	The Double Tax Avoidance Agreement
ECICA:	European Convention on International Commercial Arbitration
EU:	European Union
FDI:	Foreign Direct Investment
G20:	Twenty Developed and Developing Countries
GAFTA:	Grain and Feed Trade Association
GATT:	General Agreement on Tariffs and Trade
GDP:	Gross Domestic Product
HFCS:	High Fructose Corn Syrup
ICC:	International Chamber of Commerce arbitration
ICSID:	International Centre for Settlement of Investment Disputes
IMF:	International Monetary Fund
IPE:	International Political Economy
LCIA:	London Court of International Arbitration
LDCs:	Least Developed Countries
LMAA:	London Maritime Arbitration Association
LME:	London Metal Exchange
MAI:	The OECD Multilateral Agreement on Investment
MAP:	Mutual Agreement Procedure
MC:	Marginal Cost
MIGA:	The Multilateral Investment Guarantee Agency
MNC:	Multinational Corporation

NAFTA:	The North American Free Trade Agreement
OECD:	Organisation for Economic Co-operation and Development
OEEC:	Organization for European Economic Cooperation
PEE:	Public Economic Enterprises
R&D :	Research and Development
SCC:	Arbitration Institute of Stockholm Chamber of Commerce
UNCITRAL:	United Nations Commission on International Trade Law
UNCTAD:	United Nations Conference on Trade and Development
USDA:	U.S. Department of Agriculture
WB:	World Bank
WIPO:	World Intellectual Property Organization
WTO:	World Trade Organization

Introduction

Today, politics has an obvious effect on the distribution of wealth among various social groups, since the decisions of policy makers are decisive in all stages of the movement of goods and services, from the production process to the distribution process, and from there to the consumption process. For example, it is not possible to produce, distribute, and consume goods that the state does not allow. Again, on the point of the income generated as a result of the production process and the redistribution of this income, the political decisions of the administrative apparatus called the state are needed. For example, politicians can increase income and corporate taxes with the decisions they make, and, in this way, they can reduce the disposable income levels of individuals and institutions. Or, with a tax such as an inflation tax, individuals and institutions can seize their purchasing power at the rate of inflation. On the point of redistribution of income, it can direct production, consumption, and investment relations in the economy by distributing some of the public revenues among various individuals and groups (students, the elderly, artisans, retirees, craftsmen, farmers, investors) through political decisions. This and many other forms of practice draw attention to the oversight and control of politics over the economy. Thus, it is possible to see the direct effect of politics in all the details of life – from everyday life to social life, from income to expenditure, from public sphere to private space.

In addition to all these, politics – that is, political power – can be used as a tool for the production and distribution of wealth by individuals or groups. Wealth itself can even become a means of acquiring political power. Politicians who hold political power can direct the political economy in line with their individual interests as well as national interests. Or, they sign transactions and decisions that will contribute to the functioning of international political economy in line with the wishes of global powers. Many studies conducted in this context also support these findings. For this reason, the concepts of political economy and international political economy appear not as independent fields separate from each other, but as interdependent fields.

This book, which analyzes national and international political economy together, consists of four chapters.

In the first chapter, information is given about what political economy in general is. Then, the development of political economy from past to present is explained. It is emphasized that political economy is essentially a combination or intersection of the concepts of economy and politics, and the differences between political economy and economics are conveyed to the reader.

The second chapter examines the political economy of government regulations. This section explores the effects of policy on the economy and explains how regulatory policies can serve the personal interests of policymakers. It shows how the public economy can be used for the benefit of some but to the detriment of society as a whole. To this end, the chapter explains what capture theory is, including its process of formation and historical development. In particular, a case study on American sugar markets analyzes the effects of the government's regulatory policies on the economy, and the effects of such regulations on global welfare are investigated.

In the third chapter, a transition from political economy to international political economy is made. It is emphasized that the international political economy is a common area consisting of the intersection of national policies and the global economy. In other words, it is explained that what we call international political economy is actually the sum of international economy and international relations. Fundamental approaches that shape international political economy are discussed, including mercantilist, liberal, and structuralist approaches. In addition, the main reason for the growth of the mutual interaction between economy and politics is expressed as globalization. Thus, in this section, the concepts of globalization, global economy, and international investment are explained, and the increasing importance of the global economy in parallel with the globalization of international relations is pointed out.

In the fourth chapter, the international effects of the regulations made by countries in the legal field are analyzed, including the effects of legal regulations made for economic reasons on international relations and the international economy. The subject is thus analyzed under the heading of political economy of international arbitration. In this context, first of all, the relationships among basic concepts such as international arbitration, multinational corporation structures, and political economy are explained. In order to better understand the concept of arbitration, basic information about the definition, history, and scope of international arbitration is conveyed to the reader. Then, the formation process of the international commercial arbitration mechanism and international legal regulations on arbitration are explained. The advantages and disadvantages of the arbitration institution are discussed by comparing the alternative resolution methods and the international commercial arbitration mechanism in the resolution of international disputes. In addition, since tax problems are at the forefront of the problems arising from transnational investments, it is questioned whether the taxational arbitration mechanism can be used as an effective tool in solving the problems. In this section, which also includes resolution methods of other tax disputes, taxational arbitration practices with these methods are compared. It is shown how the arbitration practice, which is one of the main mechanisms for the resolution of investment disputes, can be applied in the area of tax disputes as well as of commercial disputes. For this purpose, taxational arbitration practices established within the scope of the Organisation for Economic Co-operation and Development (OECD) and the European Union (EU) are included.

Political economy

Chapter I Understanding Political Economy

Political economy is a holistic field of science that evaluates the interconnections between economics and political science, along with their social effects, and has been studied as such for more than 300 years. In general terms, political economy refers to the interrelationship between a country's economic and political systems. As a social science, it examines production, consumption and distribution policies and their relationship with politics. It comprises different areas of study, including national political economy and international political economy. Given the prominence that globalization and technology have reached today, it is clear that the field of international political economy has become an important discipline beyond national political economy, since in our globalizing world, international markets and political relations have gained in importance. However, political economy is not only related to politics and economy, but also integrates other disciplines within the social sciences, such as law, sociology, anthropology, and history. In this context, it uses methods and approaches such as rational choice, behavioral economics, political competition, and public choice analysis in the creation of models and analyses.

1. Getting Started with Political Economy

Before starting on subject of political economy, it is important to remember that there are basically four different areas of social life, which consist of the economic area, policy area, kinship area, and social area (Figure 1). Although the Neoclassical theory defines man as an economic being (Homo economicus, or economic man), there are areas of social life other than economy and all of these areas are related to each other. However, since the archaic period, people have used the economic field to meet their material needs and desires (biological and social needs), invent the laws of the economy, try to manage the economy, and establish economic institutions for this purpose.

In addition, people want to meet their cultural and spiritual needs. They try to maintain kinship relations and community relations (for example, family, marriage, kinship relations, work life) and establish institutions for this purpose. To this end, they build the institutional space of human relations. For example, they provide an institutional organization with structures such as the institutions of family and marriage.

On the other hand, detailed political space is needed to prevent social conflicts and implement social decisions. Because politics, the institutionalized form of power relations, the whole of relations between the ruler and the ruled, is the art of reconciling different ideas in the society. The power, which holds the political field, while inventing laws and norms to meet social and economic needs as a legislator and constructor, on the other hand, aims the order to function in a healthy way by shaping the organizational structure (bureaucratic organization-formation of institutions).

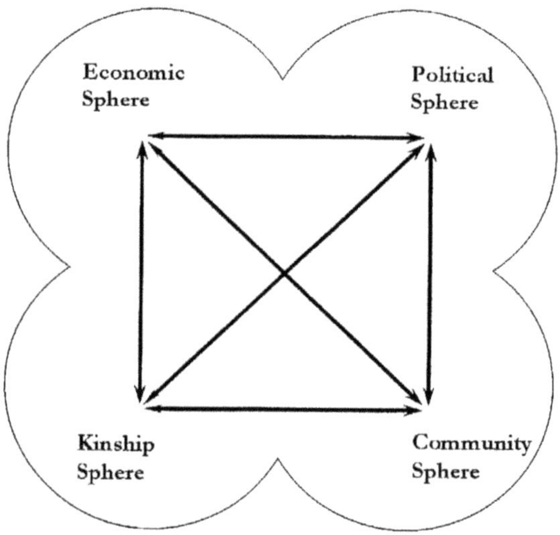

Figure 1. Four spheres of social life
Source: (Hahnel, 2014)

In that case, it is obvious that societies that fail to produce and distribute economically and cannot establish the necessary institutions in this field, the material means of life will disappear and be annihilated. Similarly, any society that cannot produce and raise the next generation in terms of kinship relations will also disappear. Again, all societies have to enter into some kind of relationship with other social communities, because these relations are necessary in terms of factors, such as sharing, cooperation, communication, and socialization. The kinship and community spheres are therefore as important as the economic sphere.

It will also disintegrate and perish in any society that cannot mediate in conflicts between members. This situation emphasizes the political sphere of social life and draws attention to the necessity of politics and its related management mechanisms. However, in this network of relations, although all areas are related to each other, it can be seen that the areas of "economy and politics" are one step ahead. Because when we look at genealogical relations and social relations, the continuation of such relations again appears as a weighted reflection of "economic and political relations". Indeed, no matter what social sphere we look at, from hunter-gatherer societies to today's societies, "economic and political decisions" are at the basis of social life. Therefore, the political economy is defined as life itself (Hahnel, 2014; Oatley, 2018).

2. Political Economy in General

The question of how politics affects economic outcomes is probably as old as the study of economics itself. In fact, what we today call economics was originally referred to – from the Physiocrats and Adam Smith's *The Wealth of Nations* (1776) at least until John Stuart Mill's *Principles of Political Economy* (1848) – as political economy. This shows that economics has always been understood as inseparable from politics, and that political factors have long been known to affect economic outcomes (Drazen, 2001).

However, the concept of political economy was first used in 1615 by Antoine de Montchrestien as a term to describe economic activities carried out within a limited scope. This early sense was later taken over by the concept of economy, while political economy came to refer to a subfield within it, though one that has the benefit of emphasizing an important aspect of the field as a whole – its interrelationship with public policy and the importance of economists in advising policy makers – and it is this feature that distinguishes the field among the social sciences (Tubaro, 2010). Classical economists such as A. Smith, D. Ricardo, and R. Malthus continued to use the concept of political economy instead of the concept of economy, generally in the period between 1750 and 1870, due to the intertwining of economics and political science. In the following period, while economic factors pushed political factors into the background, political factors also pushed economic factors into the background. As a result, it was seen that the existing disciplines progressed independently. As Tubaro (2010) notes, this situation continued until the 1929 economic depression. Along with Keynesian economic policies, appropriate approaches have emerged that allow political and economic sciences to once again meet on common ground. Factors in this period such as the expanding role of the state in economic life, the emergence and expansion of the conception of the social state, and goods and services offered by the market economy becoming demanded from the state led to the emergence of new problems in parallel with the changing role of the state in the economy. To account for these changes, new economic approaches such as public choice analysis and constitutional economics have appeared in order to analyze the effects of politics on the economy and the economy on political decision-making processes. Today, the concept of political economy refers essentially to the relationship of the economy with politics and politics with the economy. In this context, the problems that arise require a holistic evaluation as an economic-political problem. The newly emerging concept of International Political Economy (IPE) deals with the relationship between economy and politics in the international arena. Accordingly, IPE is defined as a process that deals with international relations at the intersection of economy and politics, and evaluates state policies through the mutual interaction of these two elements (Art & Jervis, 1985; Milgate & Stimson, 2011).

Understanding how politics and economics interact actually requires understanding today's world. Political decisions affect the wealth, production levels, and income distribution of individuals and groups – in short, their economies. Wealth, or the economy itself, can also be used as a way to gain political power. The search for wealth is considered probably one of the most important, if not the only, motivating factor in human behavior, and is also seen as a way to achieve other goals. On this point, it is often emphasized that politics has an important role in the formation of wealth. Bentham based human behavior on a single principle and laid the foundation for the science of happiness. He reconciled this situation with physics and mathematical truths, and from this formulated a model. According to the method developed by Bentham, benefit increases and decreases depending on many situations. According to him, people are influenced by moral rules, laws, and religious beliefs, but they look at life from a utilitarian perspective, no matter what the rules and beliefs tell them. Bentham, in his book *An Introduction to the Principles of Morality and Legislation* (1789), states: "Every man always acts everywhere with one principle, and that is to maximize his utility." He also draws attention to the fact that the entity called human is essentially a political entity as well as an economic one. According to political economy approaches, it is always possible to adapt Jeremy Bentham's rational behavior pattern based on individual interest to non-market decision-making mechanisms and the government's decision-making process, since political factors are effective in determining who will buy what, how much, and how in society. While political factors affect the economy, economic factors also affect politics. Therefore, these concepts have obvious effects on each other.

Thus Walter and Sen (2009) argue: "It is a correct approach to assume that economics and political science are closely related and even inseparable." Although this has been the case for decades, the distinction that emerged at the beginning of the 20th century led to a clarification of the boundaries, a differentiation of research problems, a change in the methods used, and the empirical divisions. Unfortunately, this situation has caused the concepts of politics and economy to be perceived as different things that do not affect each other (Milgate & Stimson, 2011; Walter & Sen, 2009).

However, even when economics first appeared with a scientific approach, it was called political economy. The main reason why it was called political economy is the coexistence of this new branch of science with the economy and the political system it is in. Every political system has a separate economic science – the economics of capitalism is, for example, different from the economics of socialism. The practice of referring to political economy as *economics* began with Alfred Marshall. After the publication of Marshall's book *Principles of Economics* in 1890, the term political economy gave way to the term economics. However, all economics books written up until Alfred Marshall are titled political economy. Incorporating mathematics and psychology into economics as tools of analysis, Marshall separated economics from ideology and politics, and transformed it into a science like physics and mathematics. As a result, the name of this field of science became economics. In fact, according to Alfred Marshall, this field of science deserved to be called economics, and the shift was even late. However, Marshall was misguided in his thinking, since although economic science is extremely intertwined with mathematics and other sciences, it has never strayed from being an ideology science, and has not been able to escape the influence of politics. Relations in the modern world are largely a product of the mutual interaction between economy and politics, so the concept of political economy can be seen as a reflection of this situation (Eğilmez, 2015; Ranney, 2000).

Political economy is a social science, and it does so using a variety of methods and tools drawn from other social sciences, such as economics, political science, and also sociology. Analyzes the relationships between individuals and society and between markets and the state. The term political economy is derived from the Greek polis, meaning "city state," and oikonomos, meaning "one who manages a estate." Political economy thus can be understood as the study of how a country is managed or governed, taking into account both political and economic factors (Veseth & Balaam, 2020).

With its focus on social relations, political economy aims to examine the power relations that affect production, distribution, and consumption, especially mutually. In general terms, the political economy is a summary of the struggle for control and survival in social life. Control concerns the ways a society organizes itself or adapts to changes, while survival is about people reproducing in order to ensure their own continuity and that of society, while thereby ensuring the continuity of production and the knowledge of how to meet the needs of society. Control processes are largely political in that they structure relations within a community. Survival processes, on the other hand, are basically economic as they relate to production and reproduction processes. Political economy emerges as a field of science that analyzes the ownership forms of the means of production, the distribution processes of societies, and the existing relations that arise in this context. Economic-political approaches pay special attention to the concept of distribution (apportionment) within the production and distribution process. Since differences emerging in the distribution process cause the emergence of class differences, it in fact explains social stratification. For this reason, it can often be seen that the political-economic perspective is used to measure income inequality (Garnett et al., 2010; Jakob, 2009; Milonakis & Fine, 2009; Mosco, 2009; Singh, 2010).

Considering the importance of political economic approaches, Vincent Mosco evaluates political economy in terms of four main areas: globalization, regulation/deregulation, unification, and digitization. Digitization refers to the emergence of computer and internet networks as the most important element of all stages of the mass communication process. The merger can be thought of as the efforts of companies to become global conglomerates and control all kinds of content, including production, distribution, and consumption, throughout the world. Regulation is the legal actions of the state to regulate the markets. Deregulation, on the other hand, aims to eliminate or reduce the regulations put forward by the state (IUORF, 2020; Mosco, 2009). Globalization, then, comprises all of the large-scale approaches aiming at the sharing and dissemination of political, technological, cultural, and social values, especially the economy, among all people by transcending national borders (Nar, 2015). All of these approaches can be said to constitute the infrastructure of political economy.

3. Development of Political Economy

Political economy, which we can define as the science of social production, distribution, and consumption relations, determines the economic laws that govern the production, exchange, distribution, and consumption of commodities. It evaluates existing relations in terms of the nature of state and market relations. With such a broad scope, the concept of political economy emerged during the development period of commercial capitalism. In the commercial period of capitalism known as mercantilism, it appears as a concept used to describe the increasingly dominant capitalist social order. With the efforts of Adam Smith to give a moral basis to the developing capitalist system, economic political approaches can also be seen to come to the fore. Smith's political economy approach – liberal political economy – legitimizes economic liberalism and opposes any outside intervention in the economy (IUORF, 2020; Veseth & Balaam, 2020). Adam Smith's Theory of Moral Sentiments (1759) marks the classical liberal tradition as one that takes seriously the ways in which the market order and the moral order intertwine with one another into a complex interdependent human system (Chamlee-Wright, 2010). According to this conceptualization, the individual who pursues personal interests also contributes to the welfare of the society he lives in by working, producing, making an effort, and earning more. The natural order that exists in the functioning of the universe also exists in the functioning of the markets, so we can speak of the natural order of the markets; since virtue is combined with human moral values such as benevolence, goodness, etc., the economy also operates according to a natural order. In this process, individuals or institutions can transfer what they have to others with benevolent donations, as well as indirectly contributing to the natural order in the form of providing job opportunities and contributing to social development. Thus, in addition to material pleasure, spiritual pleasure also emerges, since man is as much a social being as he is an individual. Human needs such as being liked, appreciated, and respected by others are as important as money. In fact, such needs can be even more important than money.

Moral side aside, Smith's views: advocacy of international specialization, based on the absolute advantage of each country, was an extension of the argument highlighting the sources of increased productivity from the domestic division of labor. Smith argued that it was better to buy abroad what was more expensive to produce at home, and exchange goods that enjoyed lower production costs at home with foreigners. However, the scope of possible international exchange between countries would be limited by whether or not they possessed an absolute advantage in a particular commodity. Smith argued that the generalized protectionism of his time was the result of "merchants' conspiracies" (interest group pressure), though he accepted that under certain circumstances protection could enhance national security (Walter & Sen, 2009).

Along with Adam Smith, economists such as Jean-Baptiste Say, David Ricardo, and John Stuart Mill laid the groundwork for the development of political economy with their studies. Apart from Marx, the common view of the economists of this period is that the invisible hand (price mechanism) has a special value that other allocation mechanisms cannot realize in the name of distribution. As a result of the exchange in the market through the price mechanism, individual welfare increases, personal interests and freedoms are protected, the producer maximizes profit, and the consumers maximize their utility. Thanks to the invisible hand in competitive markets, social welfare is maximized along with individual welfare. Since the system operates automatically, prices decrease when supply is greater than demand, and prices increase when demand is greater than supply. Provided that the property rights of individuals are respected, reconciliation (voluntary exchange) based on the principle of voluntary participation guarantees the functioning of the natural order. While the market system maximizes capital, scarce resources are effectively distributed in the economy. There is no need for an expensive bureaucratic structure to tell us what to do, just as there is no need for the state to intervene in the economy (Nar, 2020; Stiegler, 2010).

Although this is the common opinion of the economists who shaped the classical political economy, these views were sharply criticized by the German philosopher and economist Karl Marx. Marx, in his political economy studies, argued that the ideas of the ruling class are dominant in every period. According to him, relations of production are nothing but class relations, and the history of humanity is actually a history of class struggles (historical materialism). Classes that keep the material means of production at their disposal also have control over the means of mental production. Marx argued that the capitalist system is organized to exploit the laborer, and in his critique of political economy, he explained the exploitative system of the capitalist system. In this respect, Marx's work is more of a critique of political economy than an explanation of it. Emphasizing that the capitalist's capital dominates the entire national production area, Marx's statements can still be considered valid today. The dominant power/capital never does its work through tyranny. Everything is happening legally as it should be. Monetary relations are carried out completely out of the public eye and in an incomprehensible way. Political approaches stand out at the heart of distribution/apportionment relations (Dalgalıdere, 2011; Harvey, 1985).

Classical economists explain distribution relations through labor-value theory. According to them, the value of a commodity is determined by the value of the labor used to produce it (Öztürk, 2020). In this process, there is no need to talk about a problem such as income distribution, since the factors of production participating in production receive a share from production according to their marginal productivity, as is explained by Euler's Theorem (Debroy, 2004; Ghodke, 2002). Marx, though, evaluates his labor theory of value through worker-capitalist relations. He says that the value of a good can be measured by the amount of labor socially expended to produce and reproduce it. Every commodity gains value according to the amount of labor crystallized in itself. If a commodity is used in the production of another commodity, part of the labor that has been crystallized is transferred to the commodity newly produced. In the production of a new product, then, there is both labor crystallized in previously produced commodities (dead labor), and labor used in this process (living labor). However, the value of the commodity that emerges in this production process is more than the sum of the wages paid to the labor (dead and living) used in its production, since the labor force, which is commodified in the capitalist order, produces more value than its own value in the production process. To use Marx's terminology, the value of a good consists of constant capital (C) in the form of machinery, raw materials, and semi-finished products used in its production; variable capital (V) expressed as labor power; and surplus value (S). Here, only the labor factor creates value above its own value in the production process. Therefore, the labor factor is called variable capital. The total value is calculated as C+V+S. The products produced by the worker, as well as the tools that enable production, such as tools, equipment, and machinery, are products of human labor. Although the labor spent to produce the means of production is referred to by different names – buried, dead, or crystallized labor – briefly defines the concept of "capital". Living labor, on the other hand, is a concept used in contrast to dead (or crystallized) labor, and explains the labor power. According to Marx's labor theory of value, profits will fall after a certain rate because capitalists substitute dead labor (capital) for living labor (Hahnel, 2010; Koç, 2014).

Marx in the mid-nineteenth century explained the law of the falling rate of profit in his book *Capital: A Critique of Political Economy.* According to this law, the rate of profit inevitably tends to fall in the process of capital accumulation. For Marx, the source of profit is the fact that the worker produces at a level that exceeds the cost of his wage. The price of goods includes inputs and labor costs, but the value of the goods produced by the workers is more than the cost of production. If a worker works for 10 hours, and 5 hours of this work is paid for his labor, the remaining 5 hours will be the profit of the capitalist or the employer. In labor-intensive technology, the capitalist now makes a profit by confiscating the product (surplus product or surplus value). Therefore, as a result of the continuous increase in the ratio of dead capital (production tools) to live labor (labor force) in the process, the profit limit is reached at a certain point. The organic composition of capital is gradually increasing. As dead labor is substituted for living labor, it becomes inevitable for capitalism to go into crisis. The use of large and complex machines by capitalists to increase production at the same time increases the ratio of machines (capital) to workers. In this competitive environment, the labor-capital ratio is constantly growing in favor of capital. Even if productivity increases with the development of technology, profit does not increase because production is carried out using fewer workers. This is because the machinery, tools, and raw materials used in the production process, which are accepted as constant capital, do not produce a new value but transfer the value they contain to the final product. However, the only factor that produces value/profit is human labor. For this reason, even if production and efficiency increase thanks to the machine, the rate of profit decreases. As a result, there is an overall tendency towards a decrease in the profit ratio. Capitalists who want to increase profits and are constantly competing then look for ways to increase the "residual value." They thus resort to steps such as extending the working time of workers, cutting wages, and limiting benefits. In this way, the capitalist gains wealth while the workers are exploited and become victims of poverty. However, according to Marx, this system, which is based on the concept of continuous profit, will eventually destroy itself. When this will happen, though, is unclear (Beams, 2018; Dinar & Somel, 2017; Marx, 1992).

Contrary to the classical labor theory of value, Marx argued that the factors of production that participate in production do not take a real share in production, and the resulting surplus value is appropriated or exploited by the capitalists. Marx's critiques of political economy between 1830 and 1870 are actually an open critique of capitalism. However, since the late 1870s, the labor-value theory in classical political economy has given way to an understanding of value based on marginal utility. According to this approach, the value of a commodity is determined not by labor, but by the benefit it provides. Classical political economy thus pushed Marxist analysis out of the paradigm entirely, after reaching price theory. As the subject of modern economics took shape, an important distinction began to emerge between economics and political economy. Economics, in aiming to be a science with laws similar to the natural sciences, shed the political, social, and historical dimensions from its analytical repertoire, leaving it cut off from its richness and dynamism. Consequently, the political component has also been shed from the name "political economy." The science of economics has turned into an abstraction with mathematical precision – as in the natural sciences – lacking political, sociological, and philosophical elements. The mathematicalization of the field reached its present level between 1930 and 1950 (MEP, 2020; Milonakis & Fine, 2009; Veseth & Balaam, 2020).

Despite all these developments, with the emergence of Keynesian economic policies, it is seen that an understanding that allows politics and economics to meet again on common ground has come to the fore. Then, when neoliberal economic policies went out of fashion in explaining social problems, Radical Political Economy emerged as a new field of study since the 1960s. This new political economy tries to reveal the importance of politics by using the tools of modern economic analysis. It argues that economic events cannot be perceived independently of socio-political events. This is because at the basis of economic events there is a structure shaped by political and social events. In addition, people are social and political entities as well as economic entities. For this reason, to examine the problems caused by capitalism only on the basis of the economy – to present the existing problems as if they are caused by the operation of the economy itself – is, in the simplest terms, to legitimize the exploitative order.

It is clear that those who hold capital and politics also design the economy (income distribution). This situation can be explained by the Pareto Law (80/20 rule). Pareto optimal income distribution is best known as the 80/20 rule, meaning that 20 % of the population controls 80 % of the income. Vilfredo Pareto (1897) drew attention to inequality in income distribution or wealth. The rich segment, which constituted 20 % of the population in Italy, also held 80 % of the land. This rule, which Pareto found by chance over land ownership, is called the law of power. In terms of income distribution, this rule can be said to be valid today (Boccara, 2010; Bodley, 2013). Studies on the law of power have increased significantly in the past half century. According to research, it is possible to find this rule at work in all areas of life. For example, 20 % of manufactured products make up 80 % of sales, 20 % of sales provide 80 % of profit, 20 % of drivers cause 80 % of accidents, we wear 20 % of our clothes in 80 % of our life-time, and 20 % of criminals are responsible for 80 % of crimes (Boccara, 2010; Koch, 2014). The law of power is the subject of research in many sciences, particularly in economics and sociology. This approach in which Vilfredo Pareto explained the distribution of wealth or income with the law of power continues to be have current applicability. Studies on the law of power indicate that the free market mechanism tends to distribute wealth or income according to the 80–20 rule when left motu proprio. The richest 20 % of the world today receives 82 % of the world's income while the poorest 20 % receive only 1.4 %. This explicitly reveals the existence of the law of power (Small, 2011; Vogli, 2013).

As the Bundschuh (2012) put it, wealth in such a world is built only upon the poverty created. "80 % of all conventional energy sources are consumed by only 20 % of humanity." 20 % of rich people use 80 % of global financial resources. Therefore, the unfair distribution in resource consumption is also in full correlation with the distribution of poverty and wealth in the world. As Pareto points out, the struggle for income in the real world arises in the form of the domination of the minority to the majority. Political economic approaches also stand out at this point and try to make existing problems and solution proposals more visible (Nar, 2021; Stiegler, 2010).

4. Components of Political Economy

Agost Pulszky's 1888 book *The Theory of Law and Civil Society* clearly explains the political economy. According to him, "The social sciences deal with the laws governing the conditions of their rise, existence and transformation.... Political economy therefore includes the laws which govern the production, distribution and consumption of wealth" (Pulszky, 1888). However, analyses that fail to take into account the role of politics in both the preparation and operation of these laws are far from being realistic. Therefore, it is not possible to understand political economy without understanding what the concept of politics means. Politics is often defined in terms of power and authority, with power referring to the ability of an individual or group exercising it to achieve their own intended ends. Investigating who exercises power and authority, or on whose behalf they are exercised, requires understanding and analyzing political economy (Drazen, 2001).

To speak of political economy is to acknowledge that the state should intervene in economic life. The history of political economy is also of those who find the state's intervention in the economy necessary and useful; it is the history of the struggle against those who find the state's intervention in the economy unnecessary and harmful. According to the economic theory that has built up for more than three hundred years, the state every day makes institutional and legal arrangements for a number of reasons, and intervenes in the economy. Therefore, political economy basically poses the questions: What is the role of the state in the economy? and What role should the state play in the economy? Since these questions are wide-ranging, it is not possible to answer them only according to the rules of economic science. Thus, it is necessary to include political science, and perhaps other social sciences, as well as economics in the analysis of problems. Political Economics is a new branch of science that undertakes this difficult task, one that examines the laws of economic science on the one hand and those of political science on the other, and combines these laws to identify, explain, and evaluate the economic role of the state. Figure 2 shows the process of formation of political economy.

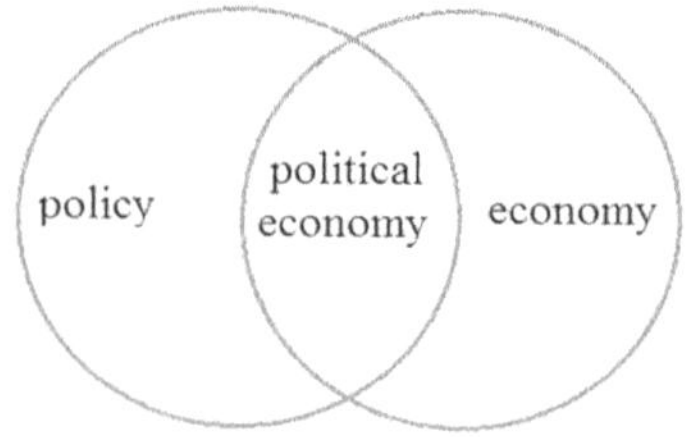

Figure 2: Political economy

In developed economies, the size of the common area or set intersection is small. It is quite large in developing countries that have not completed their industrialization. In other words, in developing economies, the relationship between politics and economy is much more expansive and important. This situation also explains why developing countries are often dragged into political depressions and crises. Most economic problems in developed countries are resolved within the existing institutional and legal framework and in accordance with economic rules. In these countries, marginal adjustments are sufficient for the economy to function well. For example, a small adjustment in interest rates or a small change in tax rates is enough to solve many problems in these economies, such as unemployment, inflation, demand-supply imbalance, and balance of payments glitches. However, structural, institutional, and legal fundamental changes need to be made in developing countries. For example, a wide range of changes should be made, such as industrialization, urbanization, value-added tax practices, land reform, establishment of public economic enterprises (PEE), minimum wage implementation, and development of a collective bargaining system. Such radical and institutional changes are often achieved through legislation. In other words, it requires the functioning of the political decision-making mechanism. This situation activates various interest groups. The relationship between economy and politics makes itself felt in every moment of daily life. That is why every economic problem in developing countries becomes a political problem, and behind every political decision there is an economic interest or loss related to one or another part of society. As Kirshner points out, behind economic and political choices there is a solid co-operation and consensus, despite all sorts of separations. This is the main reason why economic factors are mostly affected by political variables. For example, although there is little consensus in the economy about the net benefits of financial openness, especially for developing countries, countries today have and continue to implement models of financial openness due to a wide range of political preferences. For example, economic policies in many areas such as exchange rate policy, policies for the labor market, social welfare practices, corporate governance, and accounting arrangements are actually the result of political preferences. In fact, the existence of independent central banks is shown as the guarantee of liberal economies. But even central banks with the freedom to set and implement political goals cannot stray from the sphere of influence of policymakers. Therefore, an important branch of the political economy tries to explain that political preferences are actually behind such economic choices, using the language and methods of neoclassical economics (IUORF, 2020; Veseth & Balaam, 2020).

4.1. Differences Between Political Economy and Economic Science

Political economy always emphasizes that we should focus on the big picture of society. Thus, it deals with all aspects of social life together, including the political, economic, moral, and cultural. Today's political economists, such as those who belong to corporate, conservative, Marxist, Neo-Marxist, autonomist, feminist, or environmentalist schools of political thought, act with similar ideas and approaches to problems. Political economists try to explain the connection of power and wealth to cultural and social life. They also draw attention to moral philosophy. This perspective is essentially a product of the effort to create ethical and social values between economics and politics. Thus, political values aimed at greater freedom, more democracy, and more participation in political decision-making processes are put forward. In addition, in democracies, basic values such as reducing income inequality, increasing access to education, increasing employment opportunities, and setting a minimum wage worthy of human dignity are also cited. Moral values are considered together with economic, social, and cultural values (Drazen, 2001; Mosco, 2009). So, in what areas does the concept of political economy with such a wide range differ or vary from economic science?

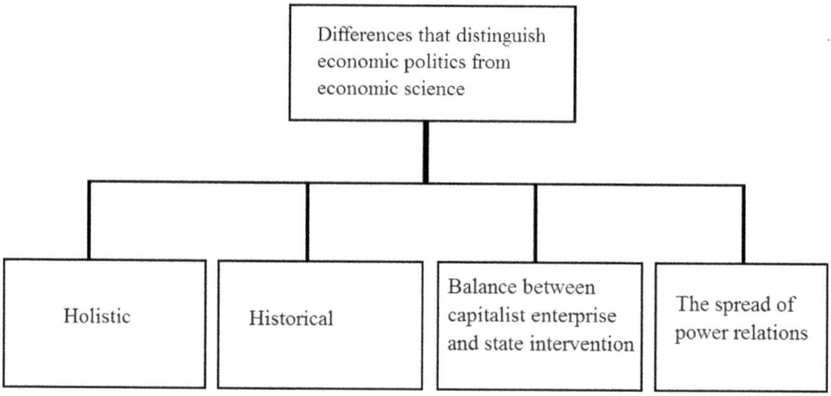

Figure 3: Differences between political economy and economics
Source: Dalgalıdere, 2011.

As shown in Figure 3, the first point of distinction between political economy and economics is that political economy analyzes existing issues with a holistic approach, unlike economics. In this regard, political economy evaluates events as a whole, not separately. Instead of individuals, it focuses directly on social relations and power relations (Dalgalıdere, 2011; Golding & Murdock, 1991; Mosco, 2009; Wasko et al., 2011). In this context, the evaluations for production processes focus on the realization of production in a way that ensures social well-being and the efficient distribution of resources in this process. In the evaluation of production processes, the level of market participation addresses the production practices for social welfare and the provision of justice. Consumption processes focus on consumption and the division of income in a way that ensures social well-being. Political economy with a holistic approach analyzes how political processes affect production and the distribution of wealth. It focuses on how political decisions affect economic activities and how they direct the benefits and costs arising from these activities.

Political economy also examines economic formations and management systems from a historical perspective. It draws attention to the role played by multinational companies (MNCs) in shaping global production and trade in the historical process. Thus, it is not possible to understand political economy without understanding the evolutionary development of MNCs. The establishment of multinational companies goes back to the 17th century. It can be said that multinational company structures emerged together with the emergence of large-scale trade as a result of geographical discoveries and colonization movements. In the 17th century, the Dutch East India Company and the enterprises operating in the North American Hudson Bay region are the first examples of multinational companies. However, none of these initiatives can be compared to today's contemporary examples. Because all of these companies were officially established by the governments of countries, their main purpose was to fund the country's treasury. The modern version of multinational corporations begins in the second half of the 19th century, when the industrial revolution reached its peak and small enterprises were replaced by large enterprises. The main purpose of the structures that emerged in this period is individual interest – in other words, profit maximization. In this process, MNCs can put pressure on the political authority of the country they visit or invest in, and they can use the current political authority to add to their profits. For example, MNCs do not face investment barriers in the host country, strict control procedures are not applied to these companies, and cross-border mergers and acquisitions can be easily realized. Besides, access to bank loans and local and foreign capital markets can be easily provided. The foreign investor has the right to a fair and even privileged benefit from the justice system. There is no limit to their use of government guarantees. There is no obstacle before the relevant companies preventing them from transfering their current profits, and they carry out such transactions without any problems. There is no restriction on their use of foreign workers. Thus, production and international trade are shaped in line with the interests and strategies of multinational companies and presented to the society.

Also, economic political approaches deal with the balance between capitalist enterprise (market economy) and state intervention (public economy). On the question of state intervention, classical political economy and critical political economy are distinguished from each other. Classics and their representatives today aim to minimize state intervention and allow the market to work as freely as possible. The critical point of view, on the other hand, differs from the classics on this point, arguing that due to inequalities and distortions in the market (market failure), the defects of the market should be corrected by state intervention.

Another issue is that the spread of power relations arises at the point of mutual interests. This issue is one of the main points of distinction between political economy and economic science. The liberal view in economics aims to reach social interests by starting from individual interests. Political economy, though, says that government policies put forward on the grounds of social interest can actually serve individual interests rather than social interests. Motivations such as being re-elected, providing political support, collecting votes, and financially benefiting are encouraging for politicians. Those who seize political power have also seized economic power along with it. In this case, political power relations become even more monetary. The spread of political relations also expands as much as possible. Therefore, political economists trying to understand domestic macroeconomic policy carefully consider the impact of political institutions – executive, legislative, and judicial powers – and the functioning of public policies carried out by bureaucratic institutions. Again, political economists focus on and analyze the role of key factors such as voters, politicians, political parties, and elections that shape the policy decision-making process. Similarly, economists such as Geoffrey Brennan and James Buchanan, who deal with economics and political science together, also explain the subject based on Gresham's law. Gresham's law says that bad money will drive out good money – in other words, bad money with low value circulates in the market, while good money with high value is withdrawn from circulation. The authors liken the behavior of politicians to this. For them, the political equivalent of Gresham's law is that "bad politicians drive out good politicians." Thus, bad politicians, in their decisions regarding the economy, serve the interests of some, rather than the interests of society as a whole. The spread of political corruption increases as much as possible. The deterioration in the political sphere is reflected in social relations, and bad behavior becomes encouraged in society. According to Segura and Braun, "all people (including good people) may turn to manipulative behavior even in the presence of a few selfish people who will govern themselves." A similar idea was put forth much earlier by William Stanley Jevons in his 1871 *The Theory of Political Economy*. So, political economy is always a living scientific field because it focuses on the vital, economic, and political interests of various layers in society. In essence, it focuses on class interests (Ibarrola, 1987; Segura & Braun, 2004).

political economy *of* regulations government

Chapter II Political Economy of Government Regulations

Political economy approaches, which emphasize the interconnectedness of economic and political systems, can be seen most clearly in the regulatory actions of governments and their activities to dominate the markets. A regulation is a set of rules or statutes pertaining to a particular jurisdiction. Regulatory actions are generally the implementation or imposition of these rules or regulations. Regulatory actions are frequently implemented by governments, especially in order to change the economic behavior of the private sector, and are supported by legal sanctions. Methods such as prices, output, profit margin, and ownership ceilings are the basic tools for regulating markets (Wild, 2006). In addition, it is possible to put into effect regulatory policies such as education and ethical standards and industry entry restrictions in order to prevent excessive competition and an excessive fall in prices, increase employment opportunities, and ensure fairer income distribution. However, the opposite concept, which should not be confused with regulation practices, is deregulation: the freeing of companies or individuals from the constraints of regulations.

The regulation of economic activities by the political powers was also seen in ancient Egyptian, Indian, Greek, and Roman civilizations. For example, standardized weights and measures were applied to some extent in the ancient world. In particular, gold and gold-based regulations were implemented in order to regulate exchange; this also allowed gold to be traded as an international currency in the relevant periods. The regulations for the national monetary system in China enabled the use of paper money in this country for the first time in the world. Again, in ancient Rome, advanced legal regulations were implemented for governing social and daily life. However, it is possible to trace the history of modern regulatory arrangements back to the mid-19th century (Braithwaite & Drahos, 2000).

The new economic order brought about by the modern age and the transformation in technology after the 1970s has also positively affected the competitive environment in the markets. This situation has created a suitable environment to meet the needs of interest groups, which come to play a role in the political decision-making process. As a result, sectors under a state monopoly, which we can define as a natural monopoly, are subject to privatization practices under the pressure of interest groups. However, the fact that the firms that won the contract as a result of the privatization of natural monopolies then re-addressed efficiency in the markets and offered a monopolistic structure once again brought the importance of regulation practices to the agenda (Posner, 1999).

1. From Politics to Economics

Various rationales have been suggested to account for economic regulation, including restraining the potential power of the market, increasing efficiency by preventing the duplication of facilities, protecting consumers, and maintaining levels of quality and ethical standards (OECD, 2008a). However, the main justification for economic regulations relates to the concept of market failure. Market failure refers to situations in which social welfare decreases when production is left entirely to market conditions. One of the main reasons for market failures is the imperfect competitive formations in the market – in other words, the existence of monopolistic and oligopolistic market structures. For example, in the presence of monopoly markets, the seller may offer his product at a monopoly price well above its cost. In the case of an oligopoly, in which a few companies dominate the market, these companies can act in the markets as they wish. In the case of a natural monopoly, opening the markets to competition leads to a waste of resources as it causes the duplication of service. Since such situations negatively affect social welfare, governments also intervene in the markets with their economic regulation policies.

Another reason for market failures is the existence of full public goods and the necessity of the presentation of these goods by the public sector. Once public goods and services are produced, the marginal cost of additional consumers consuming those goods and services is zero (MC=0). Thus, consumers cannot be excluded from consuming these goods and services. Since the price of such goods and services is P=0, it does not produce any goods with a special cut-price of zero. Therefore, the production and presentation of such goods and services is carried out by the state, or the private sector is allowed to produce, and this area is regulated by the state. For example, services such as policing, security, energy distribution, mail, transportation, etc. can today be offered by the public sector or can be offered by the private sector under certain public regulations.

The concept of externality is another factor that leads to market failure. Externality is the spread of the benefits or costs arising from production and consumption to other members of society. In markets where there are externalities, efficiency (Pareto optimal efficiency) does not occur spontaneously. Therefore, externalities need to be internalized. Externalities can be either positive or negative. Positive externalities are known as external economies. Services such as education and healthcare can be given as examples of positive externalities. The production and consumption of such goods and services externally benefits not only the individual but also the entire society. For example, societies consisting of more educated or healthy individuals are considered more democratic and more egalitarian in terms of income distribution. Negative externalities are known as external diseconomies. For example, there are negative externalities in cases such as a factory dumping its waste into a lake, an individual listening to loud music disturbing the environment, and businesses polluting the air threatening the health of the entire society. In order to eliminate negative externalities, the state can regulate the markets with practices such as high taxes, prohibition of activities, and penal sanctions. In cases where there are positive externalities, the state tries to increase production and consumption with policies such as subsidies and incentives. It can provide scholarships to students, home care fees for the elderly, and increase the number of schools. Thus, the state can either undertake the production itself in the presence of positive or negative externalities, or it can regulate these markets while allowing the activities of the private sector.

Likewise, the existence of asymmetric information problems is one of the factors that cause market failure. Such negativities also necessitate government regulations. Information asymmetry occurs when one of the parties – buyer or seller – trading in the market has more information than the other. Market failure occurs when the buyer or seller does not have equal information about the price, quality, or other characteristics of the goods and services traded in the market. In such situations, the markets do not work as they should. For example, the seller may have more information than the buyer, the borrower may have more information than the lender, the insurance company may have more information than the person receiving the insurance service, the physician may have more information than the patient, or the lawyer may have more information than the client. In all these situations, knowledge provides a competitive advantage to the one who possesses it. The conditions that make the markets work effectively disappear. Thus, in case of market failure, the intervention of the public economy in the market economy becomes legitimate and the need to regulate the markets arises (Harris & Andrew, 2011; McGivern & Fischer, 2012; Nar, 2020).

However, in practice, it is seen that government interventions or regulatory policies to prevent market failure can themselves cause negative results. Today, it is observed that government policies aimed at regulating the markets, from the most developed western societies to the least developed countries (LDCs), go beyond their purpose and cause inefficiency in the markets. Numerous examples can be found in the literature on this subject. In this way, some policies implemented by states in order to protect the public interest actually reduce social welfare – just as in market failure – instead of increasing social welfare.

Such situations can be described as government failure, a concept used to describe the negative situations that arise as a result of the state's intervention in the economy, and which is the main field of study in political economy.

Government failure can consist of:

(i) Political myopia (short-term politics)
(ii) Lack of transparency in policymakers' decision-making
(iii) A conflict of government policies
(iv) A difference between foreseen and implemented policies
(v) The existence of inefficient regulations and political forces that increase the economic rent of interest groups

Public choice theory, which analyzes the concept of government failure with an economic political approach, sees politicians as essentially people who are trying to maximize their own benefits. It thus explains that the economy cannot be independent of politics. Just as in the market economy individuals try to maximize their benefits in their specific decisions, so do politicians try to maximize their own interests rather than the social interest in their decisions (Brennan & Buchanan, 2000; Oates, 2005).

Those who oppose this view argue that politicians are people who try to maximize the public good. According to them, the main reason for the existence of the state is to maximize the public interest – that is, social welfare. Democracy itself is the basic form of government that ensures the emergence of the public interest. However, it is logical neither to define the state with the idea of infinite rationality (the public interest), as Hegel spoke of it, nor to think of it as an instrument of exploitation by the dominant classes, as Marx and Engels claimed. What is logical is that, although there is public interest at the heart of the state organization, the power that governs the state can actually intervene in the economy in a way that takes into account its own personal interests. For example, the state can directly intervene in the markets through actions such as confiscation, prohibition, privatization, and undertaking production. Or, it can intervene in the market with regulatory actions by introducing service standards, quality standards, and entry standards for sectors. Such practices aimed at regulating the markets, though, appear as economic-political approaches that clearly reveal the relations between politics and the economy.

In this section, where we refer to American political economy, it is revealed how government policies, in the form of regulations, to prevent market failures can actually create social costs. Government interventions to prevent market failures can fail, and produce inefficient results even in areas where there is no significant market failure. As well, the regulations that are purportedly made in the name of social or consumer welfare can turn into laws and economic regulations that produce economic rent for various interest groups. The costs of regulation activities are directly reflected onto the taxpayers – that is, onto the whole of society (Nar, 2020; Winston, 2006). Winston (2006) outlines some of the costs associated with certain policies in Table 1.

Table 1. Welfare Costs of Market Failure Policies (Costs)

Antitrust	The annual cost to firms that are subject to antitrust investigations and court proceedings from legal expenses and the time and resources expended by management and critical staff to assist in the defense could run into the billions of dollars.
Economic regulation	Annual deadweight losses from commodity price support programs. Annual deadweight losses from tariffs and quotas.
Social regulation: imperfect information	FTC investigations of false advertising raise firms' costs. FDA delays of the availability of new drugs have amounted to a 5–10 percent annual tax on drug purchases. OSHA inspections and regulations raise firms' costs. States' prohibitions of advertising raise prices.
Social regulation: externalities	NHTSA-mandated emissions technology raises the price of new vehicles. DOT fuel economy standards raise the price of new vehicles and compromise safety. Besides FAA noise standards are driving airlines' costs up. EPA command and control air and water pollution policies raisefirms' costs. Federally funded R&D generates low returns and crowds out private R&D. The current patent system involves large transactions costs.
Public production	Public production runs large deficits that must be covered by taxes that create an excess burden. Annual deadweight losses from inefficient pricing and investment in highways. Annual deadweight losses from inefficient pricing and investment in airports and public transit. Many inland waterway projects are not cost effective. Users of public land are charged prices below marginal cost. Prices for mail service generate inefficient cross subsidies.

Source: Winston, 2006

As a result, government interventions can be harmful. Decision makers can make political decisions to the detriment of the public in a way that benefits certain interest groups. This suggests to us that in order to understand the political economy, capture theory must be understood.

2. Capture Theory and Scope

The concept of public interest has led to the emergence of regulatory agencies. However, political economists have debated whether the idea of public interest is the main goal of these institutions. Studies show that politicians who implement regulation practices can serve their own interests instead of the public interest (Nar, 2020). Capture Theory is one of the first approaches to reveal the network of relations on this subject, and the theory begins with NPT analysis.

Until the early 1960s the prevailing theory of regulation was what Joskow and Noll have called the "normative analysis as a positive theory" (or NPT). Positive analysis refers to what is and normative analysis refers to what should be. Problems such as externalities, natural monopoly, and asymmetric information, which are considered market failures, disrupt the effective functioning of the markets. Thus, what is on the market does not always mean the same as what should be on the market. According to the NPT, the main purpose of regulatory agencies is to reduce or eliminate inefficiency caused by market failures. So, market failure is an important reason to engage in regulation. Regulation policies involve what should be in the markets, namely the concept of efficiency. However, within the scope of the NPT, some economists reveal that the reasons put forward for applying for regulation, especially the natural monopoly justification, are not very explanatory. For example, regulations regarding truck and air transport increase the gap between price and marginal cost (MC) as much as possible, and the arrangements made directly serve the interests of the company instead of that of social welfare. The regulation findings of Stigler and Friedland on electricity markets in 1962 are also extremely important in the literature. Their study shows that regulation does not lead to low electricity prices, as expected; on the contrary, prices rise in a way that serves the interests of the company rather than the social interest (Peltzman, 1989).

In 1972, William Jordan proposed a new theory called the capture theory of regulation, or CT. Jordan concluded that the inefficient regulation findings of Stigler and Friedland do not cover all types of regulation. In addition to monopoly, regulations made in competitive areas similarly increase prices and reduce the number of competitors. According to Jordan, as the NPT points out, regulation not only causes prices to rise in natural monopoly industries, but also affects other areas. The regulations serve the profits of the producer either by creating cartels or by failing to prevent a monopoly. Although the companies initially opposed the regulation, over time they found that it was in their own interests. When the entry of new firms into the sector is checked, existing firms understand that the regulation is in their own best interests, as they will continue to make excessive profits compared to competitive markets. Firms therefore provide a number of benefits to public regulatory agencies and their staff. Proponents of capture theory say that public regulatory agencies can get the public personnel they need from the regulated industry. Naturally, these people will be those who are warm to the interests of that sector. In addition, regulatory staff can transfer to such industries at high fees, or avoid conflicts of interest with companies for similar reasons. Capture theory is one of the first theories on this subject that tries to show that public regulations are inefficient, unsuccessful, and even open to abuse. Since it represents a pioneering study on obtaining private benefit from public regulation authority, it has also been the basis for subsequent studies. Thus, meaningful models can be established between the state and the business world (Peltzman, 1989; Walters, 1993).

The economic theory of regulation was put forward by George Stigler, and it is more comprehensive than capture theory. Stigler supports the theory of capture, and also argues that in his "economic theory of regulation," the regulatory institution is surrounded by economic interests. Stigler presents many model tests on how government regulation serves a firm's profit. For example, airline tariff regulations offer companies a price level that will generate greater profits than in a competitive situation. Similarly, setting minimum quality standards and limiting manufacturers to technological criteria can contribute to the profits of more established and more advanced companies. Thus, in the Stigler model, politicians increase their voting potential by moving away from the target of social benefit. Regulatory policies, meanwhile, can be bought and sold as an economic good whose price and quantity are determined depending on supply and demand in the market.

Posner opposes Stigler's argument that regulatory actions only increase the utility of producers. He states that the benefit resulting from the regulation practices is not limited to the producers, and claims that some of the benefit is reflected onto the consumers in the form of low price practices. The basic mechanism in the functioning of this structure is shown to be cross subsidization applications.

Peltzman, though, argues that the regulation practices function to maximize the benefits of both the consumer and the producer, as well as the politicians responsible for the regulation practice (Peltzman, 1989; Viscusi et al., 2005; Walters, 1993).

A concept similar to the theory of capture is public choice theory. As with the theory of capture, public choice says that the pattern of behavior based on individual interest exists among actors involved in the political economy. The main elements that guide the theory can be listed under three headings: rationality

(Homo economicus), methodological individuality, and catallaxy. Since classical political economy, economists have been interested in issues related to people's individual preferences – namely, their behavior in the market. However, the focus solely on individual preferences in the markets restricts economic approaches, which also makes it difficult to understand out-of-market decision-making mechanisms, such as politicians, bureaucrats, interest groups, voting, etc. Similarly, the new corporate economy (micro-economic approaches) draws attention to the need to examine people's reactions in the real world more closely, and emphasizes the importance of the concept of rationality. According to the concept of rationality, the individual pursuing personal interest is rational in his behavior, and tries to maximize his utility. According to the theory, the concept of rationality also exists among the actors involved in political economy, and this is undeniable. The second important concept is methodological individuality. The main idea here is that, as in the market economy, decisions made in the public economy are determined entirely according to individual preferences and there is no difference between them. Methodological individuality is also the cornerstone of public choice analysis. It focuses on individual preferences that are ignored by non-market mechanisms. Thirdly, the concept of catallaxy is based on the idea that politics is actually a kind of exchange, and the term is used to describe the order caused by mutual exchange. Just as goods and services produced in the market economy are subject to exchange, goods and services produced in the public economy are actually also the subject of exchange. However, while "money" is the basis for exchange in market economy, "voting" serve a similar function in public economy (Krichner, 2007; Rowley, 2008).

In addition, regulations always tend to be in demand by well-organized interest groups seeking to guard against market competition. Research has shown that interest groups generally consist of small units, and their information and communication costs – which we can define as bargaining costs – remain extremely low. However, according to a famous thesis dating back to James Madison, a federative (decentralized) structure can also reduce the power of interest groups. In addition, unions and the centralization of consumers in associations also weaken the ability of interest groups to organize, since in this case, the costs of obtaining information, communication, organizing, and lobbying for interest groups increase. Thus, the collective benefits that group members can internalize are also reduced. According to capture theory, just as company managers are tasked with increasing the profits of the partners, politicians and bureaucrats are similarly tasked with increasing the profits of interest groups. Just as company executives gain additional power to the extent that they increase the company's assets and maintain control, bureaucrats and politicians have significant political power to the point where they receive the support of interest groups. Therefore, this general relationship among bureaucrats, politicians, and pressure/interest groups is extremely important in determining the political balance. Thus, a small political minority, due to the high costs of obtaining and organizing accurate information, is able to easily manage the majority, namely the people (Bernholz & Vaubel, 2007; Stigler, 1971).

3. Application of Capture Theory to US Sugar Markets

Discussions of government regulations generally take the existence of the public interest as a starting point, and have a political character. However, the costs and benefits imposed on society by government regulations can be analyzed economically. For this reason, political economists consider regulation policies with a holistic approach, analyzing them in terms of both economics and political science. As a case study, in this section, regulations regarding the US sugar markets are discussed with an approach incorporating both politics and economics. Regulations for sugar markets are analyzed within the scope of capture theory, as it is a clear example of policy-making attempts at rent-seeking.

Detailed information on the subject is obtained from the article titled *Effects of Regulatory Authorities on Sugar Markets: An Evaluation on the USA Case*, published in the *International Journal of Contemporary Economics and Administrative Sciences*. The analysis is presented to the reader as a clear example of how regulatory agencies can serve personal interests rather than social interests (Nar & Nar, 2020).

Regulations for the US sugar markets have led to the widespread use of high fructose corn syrup, which we can describe as the plague of the age. High fructose corn syrup production in the US, which is increasing daily, has reduced sugar imports and has made significant contributions to the economy with its undisputed role in the food sector. However, at the same time, the increase in chronic diseases and chronic health expenditures in the US has emerged as an important social problem that needs to be addressed.

Regulatory authorities are independent structures organized in the form of supreme boards. The concept of public interest led to the birth of public regulatory authorities. However, economists have debated whether the public interest is the main objective of such institutions (Kothari, 2010). In practice, the first examples of these institutions were found in the US, where the Interstate Commerce Commission was established in 1887, and the Federal Trade Commission was established in 1914, for the prevention of unfair competition. The search to find a judicial solution to administrative problems in the US, where an administrative jurisdiction organ did not exist, resulted in the emergence of these structures (Lust, 1927; Sever, 2015). Similar institutions were established in Europe in the 1980s (Davis & Abraham, 2013), and in Turkey after the 1990s. The main debate concerns the fact that these institutions, which are in charge of regulation and supervision, act to serve individual interests rather than the social interest, because first politicians and then companies and bureaucrats can make legal regulations according to their own interests in order to ensure rent. In the literature, it is possible to find numerous examples supporting these findings (Milgrom & Roberts, 1998). Findings that regulatory authorities can serve individual interests rather than the public interest were first noted in the 1960s with the theory of regulation by Joskow and Noll. The studies in this area were carried out in in accordance with capture theory (CT), which had been ignored in the literature. Findings have shown that regulatory activities conducted in non-competitive markets, such as natural monopolies, can actually serve individual interests rather than the public interest.

This case study analyzed the effects of regulatory authority activities on health economics. For this purpose, the focus was placed on the sugar market, which is one of the markets most affected by regulatory activities. The study tried to explain how high fructose corn syrup (HFCS), a flavoring substance, became widespread in the market. Additionally, the effects of HFCS production and consumption on chronic diseases and the economic costs of these diseases were discussed.

3.1. Literature Review

In the 1960s, regulatory measures in the areas of trucking and air transportation increased, rather than reduced, the overall level of prices. Similarly, while regulatory actions in the US electricity market were expected to lead to lower electricity prices, they actually increased the overall level of prices. In addition, regulatory authorities established to control water pollution can serve the interests of companies instead of preventing the harm caused by industry on the environment. As a result, regulators can cause further inefficiency rather than preventing inefficiency caused by market failure (Peltzman, 1976; Stigler, 1971).

As of the 1970s, the concept of market failure gave way to the concept of government failure. Neoliberal policies gained ascendancy, and the role of the state was once again questioned. The development in technology and in the financial markets during this period positively influenced the competition environment. This, in turn, created an environment suitable for the needs of interest groups. First, the areas under state monopoly, which would be defined as natural monopolies, are exposed to privatization by the pressure of interested groups. Firms that buy these institutions as a result of the privatization of natural monopolies show efforts to become powerful in the market. The regeneration of these companies as monopolistic structures once again shines a light on the regulations (Posner, 1999).

In 1972, William Jordan described this situation with the capture theory of regulations (capture theory or CT). In addition to monopolies, regulative actions in competitive markets increase prices and reduce the number of competitors. George Stigler, who introduced the theory of economic Regulation in 1971, stated that regulatory authorities are surrounded by economic interest. For example, the regulation of airline tariffs or the introduction of minimum quality standards for new firms reduces social welfare while contributing to company profits (Joskow & Noll, 1981). Capture theory is the first theory on the subject that shows that public regimes are unproductive, unsuccessful, and even vulnerable to corruption. It also became the basis for subsequent studies, since it can be considered the first study in the literature on deriving personal benefit from the public regulatory authority. Thus, it is possible to establish meaningful models based on the interests between the state and the business world (Walters, 1993).

The U.S. Food and Drug Administration's federal regulations limit competition and increase costs in cases where there are no regulations, which in turn reduce investments (Baker et al., 2008). As a result, the costs incurred by regulatory authorities are paid by individuals – i.e., taxpayers. This causes a decrease in the disposable income of individuals. Less income means less safety, less health, less education, less nutrition, less housing, and a lower quality of life – all of which make life riskier for individuals. Statistically, the expense that the regulator created in this field is more than $14 billion. This cost requires the regulatory agencies' areas of activity to be redefined to reflect the public interest (Keeney, 1997; Nar & Nar, 2019).

The US Department of Transportation's gasoline mileage regulations applied between 1981 and 1984 were investigated in terms of economic efficiency and equity. According to these regulations, low-income groups with fewer cars were exposed to inequality compared to higher-income groups. Attempts were made to compensate low-income groups who experienced losses by additional income compensatory measures. Food stamps, fuel stamps, supplementary gasoline, low-income family assistance coupons, and discounts in income tax rates were applied within this context. However, these measures did not reach the intended goal (Lakhani, 1980). After sulfur dioxide emission regulations were applied in the US between 1975 and 1990, electricity production costs, which should have decreased, actually increased by 1.1 %, resulting in consumers receiving higher bills (Lee, 2002).

The aim of the regulations in banking is to reduce financial fragility, prevent economic crises, provide stability, build competitive financial markets, strengthen public audits, and provide capital adequacy. However, it was found that regulations introduced to banks to increase financial security – e.g., deposits being listed under insurances, bank rescue operations – contributed more to the instability of the banks and increased existing risks (Allen & Gale, 2004; Demirgüç & Detragiache, 2002).

The results of the regulations were directly reflected in the taxpayers' budgets. This may result in an excessive interruption of Medicare premiums, a high rate of taxation on wage income, a decrease in the payments to people in need, a reduction of meal allowances, and the cancellation of housing assistance, etc. The IMF's economists have calculated the size of these implicit subsidies as $83 billion (Herbst, 2013; Valdez & Molyneux, 2015).

The basis of the problem is foreseeing that the regulatory and supervisory authorities are rational institutions that act in the public interest. Unfortunately, a great number of regulatory activities are carried out for either personal interest or political interest. For example, labor force costs and minimum wage regulations can be determined according to the interests of companies. In the current market conditions, the rules are made flexible, and unions are made inactive. Similarly, agricultural regulations continue to benefit a minority of people, preventing the application of sustainable public policies (Mesquit, 2017; Pawłowski, 2009).

A clear example of this is US sugar regulations. These regulations can be addressed in three separate periods. The first period is between 1789 and 1890, during which sugar production was not significant, and thus protection was not required. However, customs duties were applied in order to create income from sugar imports. The second period after 1890 is when import tariffs were removed to facilitate a high level of sugar intake, and domestic sugar processing factories were supported by the incentives. The period beginning in the 1930s is the third period. In 1934, the Sugar Law was established to protect the domestic industry, due to increased sugar production and falling prices. This law limited the import and production of sugar. The Sugar Law was terminated in 1974 because sugar prices in the world increased by approximately three times that year. In 1977, a new protection policy was introduced into the sugar industry as a result of increased production and falling prices, and a regulatory authority was established under the name of the Commodity Credit Corporation (CCC). In the face of falling prices, support for producer prices as well as credit programs were put into practice. These arrangements became permanent with the new Agricultural Law of 1981. Many changes in the year 2000 were carried out by the CCC to prevent the accumulation of sugar stocks in the US. In particular, payments in kind, as well as cash payment programs, are important for producers, in exchange for restriction of the cultivation areas. In this respect, it was possible to reduce the cultivation areas by 7–10 % (Grossmann, 2012; Kıymaz, 2002; USDA, 1996).

The main regulatory agency in the US sugar market is the Department of Agriculture (USDA), which determines the legal framework of the relevant public policies (IEG Vantage, 2018). Another institution operating in this area as an independent regulator is the Commodity Futures Trading Commission (CFTC), which regulates and controls the commodity markets. These markets include traditional agricultural products such as sugar, wheat, corn, and soybeans, as well as nonagricultural products such as precious metals (CFTC, 2018). The aim of these institutions is to protect the rights of US farmers and businesses, and ensure that they can continue their activities in fair terms in the global markets (Landis, 1987; Winden, 2004). Nowadays, US sugar regulations are carried out under the context of price support to domestic producers. In addition, low-interest loans, payment in kind, and down payment arrangements are in place, and price and quantity quotas for foreign products are applied when required. The importance of sugar is governed by tariff-rate quotas under the North American Free Trade Agreement (NAFTA) and the Uruguay Round Agreement (USDA, 2018). Nevertheless, agriculture subsidies in the US are extremely unproductive transfer programs. The annual cost of price support programs – i.e., subsidies – under economic regulations is between $12.4 billion and $30 billion. Moreover, the loss created by quotas and taxes is between $12 billion and $18 billion. Therefore, in sugar markets, self-interest conflicts with the interests of the public, which in turn hinders social welfare (Nar, 2020; Tullock et al., 2002).

The USDA has stated that, in the event of sugar stocks becoming inadequate, it can intervene in the sugar markets to prevent an increase in sugar prices (Mueller, 2011). However, it is not known for whom or why these limitations were introduced or removed. At this point, interest-based relations among (i) politics, (ii) bureaucracy, and (iii) businessmen emerge. This triple structure is referred to as the "iron triangle," and directly targets the activities of the regulator. At the end of the day, politicians who are regarded as acting in the public interest are actually pursuing vote maximization. It is understood that those who establish regulations are striving for bureaucratic maximization. It is also recognized that interest groups that are composed of business people wish to seize public resources through lobbying activities. Along with the numerous corruption cases in Western democracies, the prevalence of interest groups in the US supports these evaluations (Mueller, 2011; Yandle, 2001).

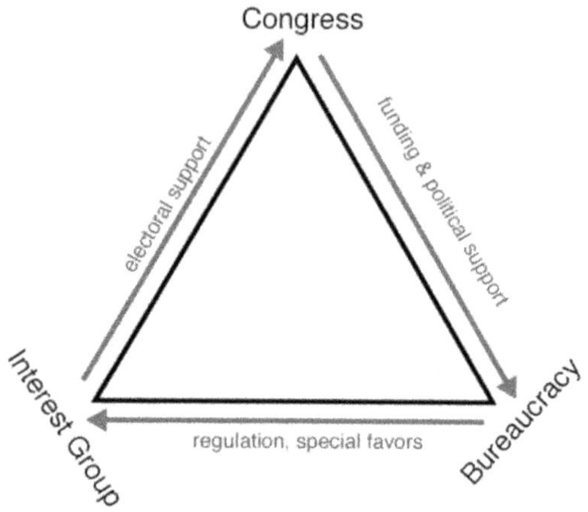

Figure 4: The Iron Triangle
Source: Iron Triangles, 2018.

Figure 4 shows the actors involved in policy-making processes, namely (i) congressional committees, (ii) the federal bureaucracy, and (iii) interest groups. While these actors aim to maximize their profits within the political process, their interest-based relations are as follows: (i) congressional committees provide financing and political support to the federal bureaucracy and maximize their budgets. The bureaucrats who manage the agencies get power and income opportunities, and their prestige increases in society. (ii) The federal bureaucracy provides the interest groups with the necessary arrangements in line with the wishes of Congress. (iii) The interest groups transfer part of the profits they earn to Congress members in the form of donations or help, and offer support for elections through lobbying (Burstein & Linton, 2002; Iron Triangles, 2018).

One of the areas where this is often experienced is the Department of Agriculture. The three-dimensional structure is particularly evident in the agricultural sector. Legislative committees are the most important part of this frame. Both in the Senate and in the House of Representatives, from allocations to quotas and tariffs, there are strong agricultural committees that present existing arrangements in favor of interest groups. These committees are "spending serious money to prevent declines of prices in the market." For example, sugar is expensive in the US. This is due to a successful pressure group composed of groups of small sugarcane producers. Sugarcane does not grow well in most parts of the US. Although it is possible to supply sugar from other sources, a small but successful pressure group prevents imports; thus, a special monopoly occurs. As stated by Tullock, "a large part of the earnings is in the hands of lobbyists and a small number of large farm owners." The amount transferred to the other farmers is around $1 billion and is an extremely small slice of the cake. The resulting costs are not limited to consumers and taxpayers. This turns into a diseased structure that affects the whole society in the form of negative externality in the long run (Pawłowski, 2013; Tullock, 1989; Tullock, 2007).

3.2. Material and Methods

First, the theoretical framework was prepared by conducting a detailed literature review on the research question. In doing so, the significance of the study and why the research question was worth studying were explained. The data used in the study were shown in metric tons. The difficulty of reaching the data as well as the classification of the data according to different weight units constituted the difficulties and limitations of the study. The fact that the weight units have been indicated in terms of pounds, short tons, and metric tons for different years made the calculations difficult. For this reason, calculations were made by converting them into the most useful method, namely metric tons. No studies were found in the literature that presented all the data together in metric tons. Thus, the data were presented in a uniform manner to facilitate future studies.

Within the scope of the study, the data provided by the USDA and the US Department of Health and Human Services were compiled and transformed into tables and graphs. Correlation analysis (SPSS 20) was then used to determine whether there was a significant relationship between the variables and the degree of the relationship, if any. Statistical analyses were performed at a confidence level of 99 %.

3.3. Results

3.3.1. Sugar Markets and HFCS

Interest or pressure groups can intervene both directly and indirectly in political decision-making processes. These groups are able to change legal arrangements according to their self-interests and undertake rent-seeking activities. This is an important social as well as economic problem that has become a major dilemma in the US, where lobbying activities are legal (Congleton & Hillman, 2015; Lambsdorff, 2002). Assessing the problem in terms of sugar markets will help in the understanding of the seriousness of the issue.

When the history of the sugarcane plant is reviewed, we see that it first originated in New Guinea. It is thought to have spread to the Southeast Asian islands more than 2000 years ago. Later, it reached China, India, and the Middle East, where refining techniques were used to transform the juice of the cane into sugary solids used in culinary applications. It then began to be grown in the Mediterranean region, especially in the south of Spain and in Sicily (Richardson, 2009).

The first production of sugar plants in the US began in Florida in 1850, but sugarcane production and its processing industry could not develop because of the geographical proximity to Cuba. However, due to the embargo imposed after the revolution in Cuba, production has been growing rapidly since 1960. Sugar ultimately became a political product under protection, as the by-product of processing, in addition to its contributions to production and employment over the following years (Kıymaz, 2002; OECD, 1998).

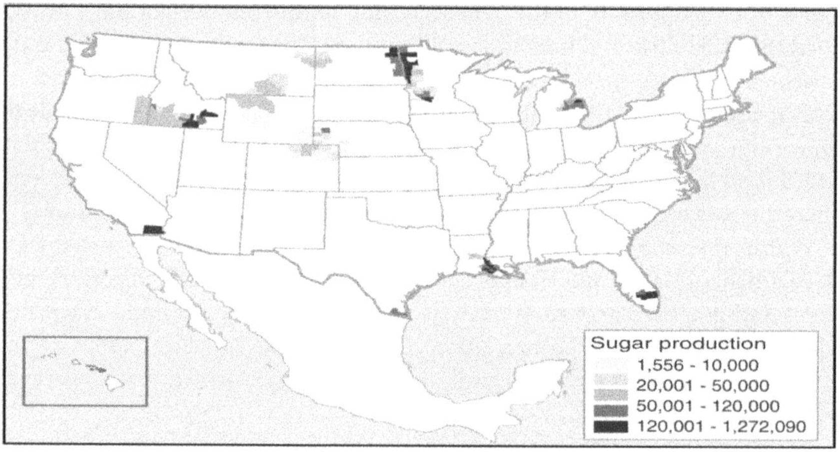

Figure 5: US production of sugar from sugar crops (1,000 metric tons)

Source: USDA, 2018. Sugar is produced in five US regions encompassing 14 States. The leading sugar producing regions are in red.

Figure 5 shows the limited sugar cultivation areas in the US. Sugar beets and sugarcane are the two primary agricultural commodities used to manufacture sugar in the US. The crop quantity that can be taken from the soil is shown in metric tons.

The fact that sugar is expensive throughout the world has facilitated the emergence of alternative profitable substances. In the five years during which two major price increases took place in the middle of the second half of the 20th century, namely in 1975 and 1980, turbulence was experienced in sugar production. From the 1960s until today, retail sugar prices have increased by six times. This has rapidly expanded the market share of sugar-like products. This enlargement was clearly observed during those years in developed countries such as the US and Japan, where the demand for sugar increased, while imports decreased (Kıymaz, 2002; White, 2014). The main reason for the reduction in imports was the existence of a "very successful, small pressure group which prevented imports" (Tullock, 1989). Problems regarding political instability and sugarcane production areas, as well as government interventions, caused a reduction in sugar supplies and an increase in prices. As a result, the current problems have primarily affected food and beverage producers, and led them to seek new solutions. Within this context, the production of HFCS emerged in the US. In this respect, a new area of use for corn was established, because it is the most grown crop in the US (Pomeranz, 2016; White, 2014).

Essentially, the process of obtaining sweet substances from the starch of products such as corn, potatoes, and wheat dates back to the beginning of the 1800s. In 1811, the conversion of starch into a sweet substance by heating it with diluted acid was carried out by Russian chemist G.S.C. Kirchoff. In the US – the country that produces the most syrup from starch today – the first plant to produce syrup from starch was established in 1831. Until the 1970s, starch-based sweeteners were produced at an insignificant level. However, at the end of the 1970s and in the early 1980s, the use of processed food products, especially by US beverage companies, increased significantly, causing this field of production to grow significantly. Due to the fact that corn is the most important cereal product grown in the US, syrup production from corn starch has become particularly common. The increase in HFCS production is almost certainly in parallel with the increase in population and consumption (BeMiller & Whistler, 2009; Taubes, 2007; Bracking, 2009).

After the year 2000, HFCS production in the US increased its market share in the sugar sector by more than 45 %, with an average production of 8.5 million tons. Japan and Canada followed the US in terms of production amount. HFCS production in the world is around 12.5 million tons. In Turkey, at the end of 2010, it was approximately 400,000 tons. The European Union (EU) is the third largest sugar producer and the second largest consumer in the world. The use of HFCS in the EU has been limited due to the quotas of an average of 2 % (EU Sugar Policy, 2018; Karaoğlu, 2011).

As can be seen in Figure 6, sugar production in the US exceeded eight million metric tons in the year 2000. US domestic producers have been protected from low world prices even during times when sugar production increased and world prices dropped, with methods such as price supports, import restrictions, and production controls. When prices around the world were high, the US government removed production limits. However, US sugar regulations have caused domestic prices to rise further and more significantly than those in the rest of the world. The consumption of sugar in the US peaked in the mid-1970s, exceeding nine million metric tons. In the late 1970s, however, consumption decreased, and this decrease continued throughout the 1980s. The main reason for this was the beverage sector's shift to HFCS. In addition, domestic consumption increased during the 1990s and early 2000s, due to increases in the bakery, confection, and other food industries (Wiltgen, 2007).

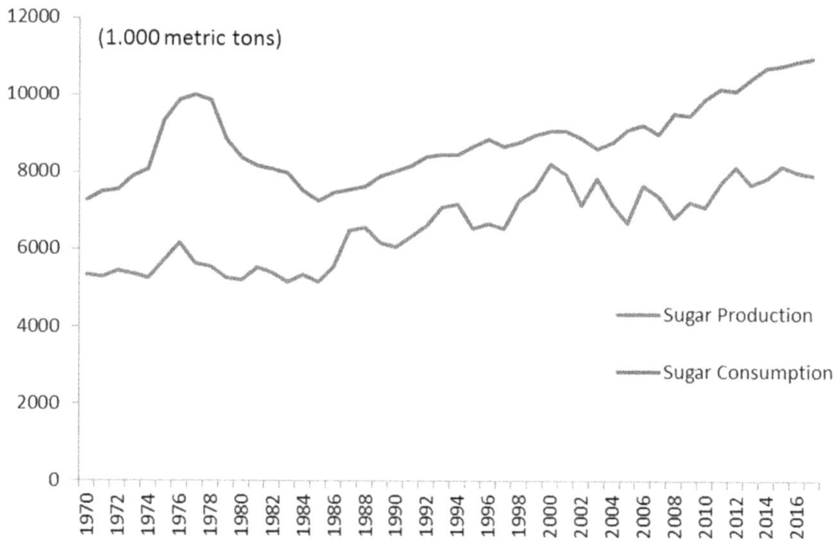

Figure 6: Sugar production and consumption in the US

Source: USDA-Economic Research Service. The amount of sugar production and sugar consumed in pounds and short tons were converted into metric tons. One metric ton (or ton) equals 1,000 kilograms or a unit of weight equal to approximately 2,204.6 pounds. One short ton (US) equals 0.907 metric tons. The data is compiled by the authors and can be quoted with reference to it.

A correlation analysis was performed to examine the relationship between sugar production and consumption, and the Pearson correlation coefficient was obtained. Accordingly, a positive correlation of 66.2 % was determined between production and consumption (r = 0.622, p <0.001).

		Sugar Consumption (Thousand tons)
Sugar Production (Thousand tons)	r	.662**
	p	.000
	N	48

**. Correlation is significant at the 0.01 level (2-tailed).

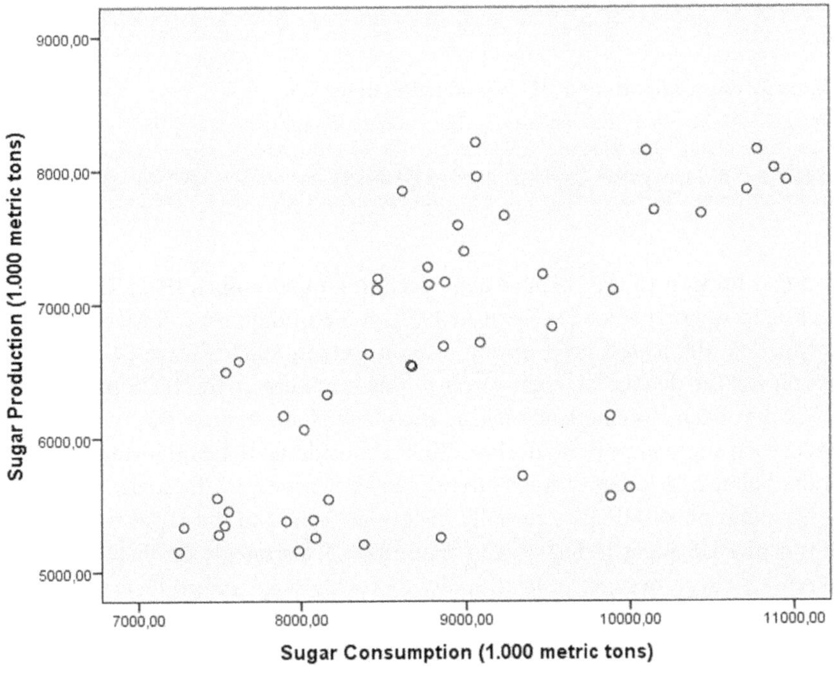

Graph 1: Sugar production and consumption in the US

The positive dispersion relation between the two variables is shown above with the aid of a scatterplot (Graph 1). As a result, an increase in sugar consumption due to the increase in population and income also spurred an increase in sugar production (Barry et al., 1990).

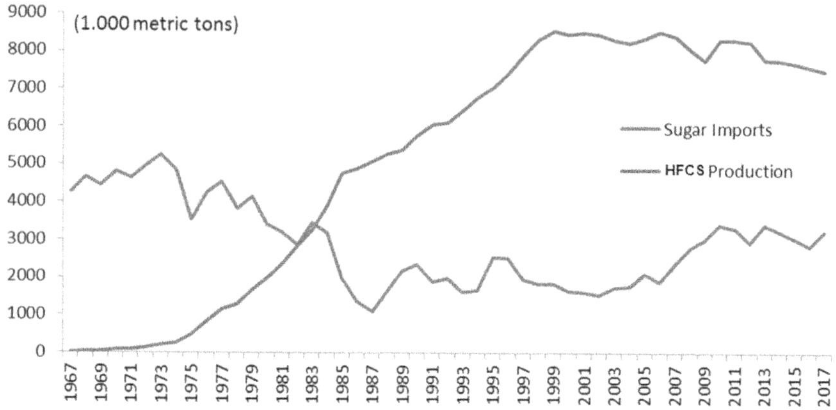

Figure 7: Sugar imports and HFCS production in the US

Source: USDA-Economic Research Service. The amounts of sugar imports and HFCS production in pounds and short tons were converted into metric tons. One metric ton (or ton) equals 1,000 kilograms or a unit of weight equal to approximately 2,204.6 pounds. One short ton (US) equals 0.907 metric tons. The data is compiled by the authors and can be quoted with reference to it.

Sugar imports in the US have been declining rapidly since 1975. The greatest decline in imports since 1967 was in 1982, at 2.8 million tons. Imports of sugar dropped to the lowest level of one million tons in 1987 (Figure 7). The main reason for the decline in sugar imports was the increase in HFCS production. HFCS has been systematically taking the place of sugar since the 1970s, which has caused sugar imports to decline. This is considered to be important in terms of the balance of foreign trade (Jurenas, 2004; Schmitz & Christian, 1993). The rapid adoption of HFCS, especially in the 1980s, led to the rapid transformation of the US sugar industry. This made HFCS a strategic product compared to refined sugar, because of its usability in a wide range of products in place of sugar, the convenience of its use in soft drinks, and its lower production costs (Barry et al., 1990). That is why almost half of the caloric sweeteners in the US are produced from corn syrup (Mitchell, 2005).

Although the relative decline in HFCS production after the year 2000 is considered to be true, this is mainly related to the use of corn for increased ethanol production. In addition, as health-conscious consumers moved toward fresh and unprocessed foods, the industry demand decreased. Despite all of this, efforts to substitute HFCS for more expensive sugar were rapidly put in place (IBISWorld, 2017; McConnell, 2017). The correlation analysis results of the present study also support the existing findings.

		HFCS Production
Sugar Imports (Thousand tons)	r	–.763**
	p	.000
	N	51

A negative significant correlation was found between sugar imports and HFCS at 76.3 % (r –0.763; p <0.001). When HFCS production increased by one unit, sugar imports fell by 0.763 units. The existence of the negative dispersion relation between the variables appears in the scatterplot as follows (Graph 2):

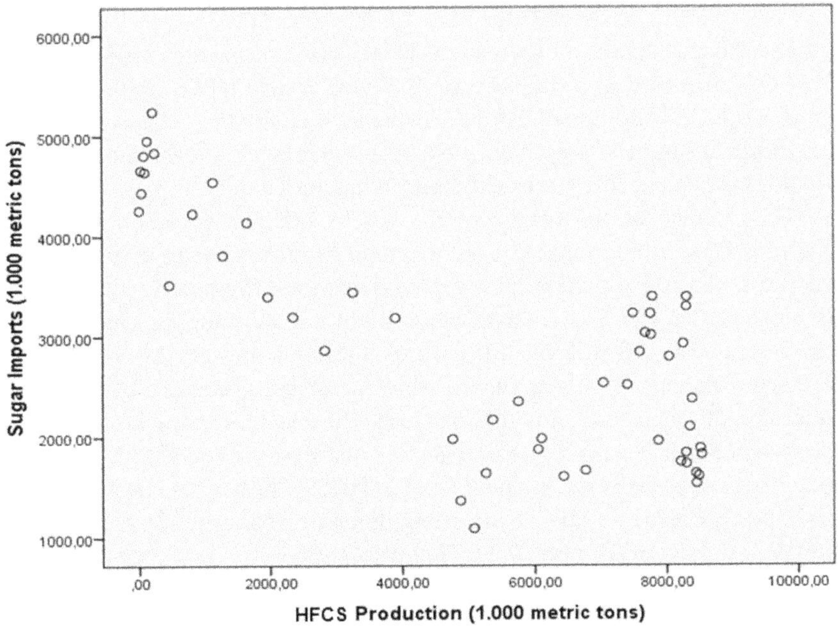

Graph 2: Sugar imports and HFCS production in the US

When assessed in general terms, the reasons for sugar costs being high in the US – in addition to the influence of environmental factors, since the climatic conditions are not well-suited for sugarcane cultivation in most of the US – are mainly due to federal sugar regulations. These regulations include tariffs, import quotas, and purchasing programs to protect domestic sugar producers against global competitors. Although these regulations create a relatively stable price level regarding the world market prices, they always create higher prices. For instance, in 2013, the price of refined sugar in the US was 66.02 cents/pound, compared to 22.84 cents/pound in the world markets. At the same time, the price of HFCS was 38.64 cents/pound, almost half the price of sugar in the US. This is the main reason the consumption or use of HFCS in the sweetener sector has increased so much today. The market share of HFCS was only 5 % in 1975 but rose to 44 % in 1989, and today this percentage is nearly 50 %. Nevertheless, non-official figures emphasize that the HFCS use rates are well above this level (Ma et al., 2014; Schmitz & Christian, 1993).

3.4. The Plague of the Age and Its Effects on Health

In step with the significant increase in HFCS production, the consumption of HFCS has increased in a similar way. The number one HFCS producer in the world is the US. Additionally, the US is the second largest HFCS consumer in the world after India (Barry et al., 1990; Korves, 2011). Thus, the most relevant questions are: What is HFCS exactly? and What does it do?

HFCS, known as the plague of the age, is different from normal sugar (Wellness Tips, 2007) in that it is not a natural substance but an industrial food product. It consists of a chemical compound extracted from corn stalks through a secret process. HFCS contains harmful and toxic substances including mercury, because the chlorine alkaline used in extracting the corn extract contains mercury. Cane sugar or beet sugar – that is, sucrose – consists of two sugar molecules, 50 % glucose and 50 % fructose. The enzymes in the human digestive system break down sucrose into glucose and fructose and absorb it into the body. These rates, however, are not 50–50 in HFCS. The fructose ratio is around 80–90 %, which makes HFCS something different from a nutrient. What it is, though, is unknown (Hyman, 2011; Pleunie, 2017).

Corn syrup is used as a thickener, sweetener, and moisturizer, especially in commercial foods. With the addition of corn syrup, products are able to maintain their freshness for long periods of time (Varzakas et al., 2012), they are more durable than traditional products, undesirable crystallization is inhibited, disadvantages such as adhesion and deterioration in packaging are eliminated, and products become easier to store and move. The most important advantage of HFCS is that it is 1.8 times sweeter than sugar and is produced 50 % more cheaply (Brown, 2019; Pleunie, 2017).

The fact that HFCS performs the same function as normal sugar makes it possible to commercially substitute the two substances with consumers hardly noticing the difference. It is critical that HFCS does not have a different flavor when it replaces sugar. That is why, in the US and Canada, almost all non-alcoholic beverage and syrup producers have shifted from sugar to HFCS (Varzakas et al., 2012).

It is clear that the increase in HFCS production has contributed significantly to the US economy. The added value of HFCS production in the last 20 years is 2.0 % of the annual average of gross domestic product (GDP). It is estimated that this ratio will increase to 3 % in the next 10 years. However, the increase in chronic health expenditures along with the increase in HFCS production is more striking. In 1998, expenditures on chronic health issues reached 9 % of the GDP in the US. By 2018, this share increased to 14 % (IBISWorld, 2017; Statista, 2018). Therefore, the economic gain obtained from HFCS production can turn into chronic diseases and social costs resulting from the consumption of HFCS. As supported by the current findings, considered together, these costs surpass the economic gain.

The term chronic diseases is used for diseases that require long-term care and are very difficult if not impossible to recover from (Dalal, 2000). Such diseases are caused by a number of factors, such as genetics, the environment, psychology, and nutrition. The share of HFCS in nutritional-based chronic diseases is prominent. Fructose, a stronger sweetener than glucose, is absorbed very quickly into the blood circulation, unlike sugar. After it reaches the liver, it is converted into triglycerides – that is, fat. This is the main cause of liver damage and fatty liver. HFCS has also been proven to cause many other illnesses including tooth decay, diabetes, heart disease, cancer, dementia, and obesity. Thus, HFCS is a subject that should be carefully evaluated in terms of its costs on health (Hyman, 2011; Lustig, 2013).

In the US, the share of healthcare in the economy is increasingly growing, which means a greater economic activity compared to other sectors. For example, sectors such as education, transportation, and agriculture develop in line with economic growth, yet healthcare costs grow at a higher rate than the average (KFF, 2012). To illustrate this, total health expenditures in the 1970s were around $74 billion, and health expenditures per capita were only $355; however, in 2016, total health expenditures reached $3.3 trillion and health expenditures per capita increased to $10,000. In other words, while the share of health services in economic activities was 6.9 % in the 1970s, it reached the very high level of 17.9 % in 2016. As Figure 8 shows, chronic health expenditure per capita, which was $266 in the 1970s, rose to $7,176 in 2016 (HealthData.gov, 2018; Peterson, 2018). The increase in chronic health expenditures in parallel with the increase in the consumption of HFCS is striking.

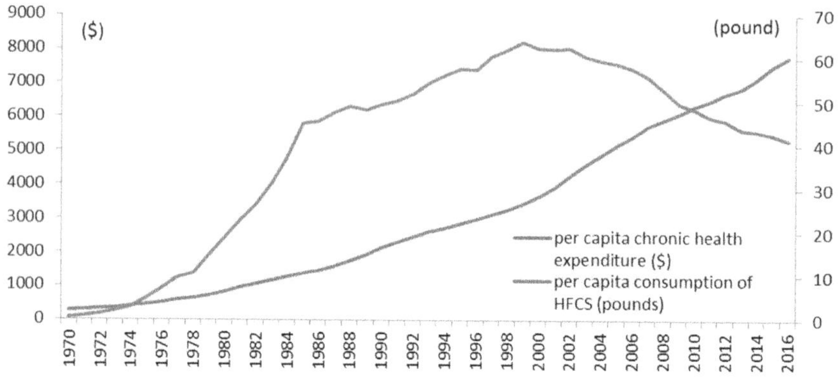

Figure 8: HFCS consumption and chronic health expenditures in the US

Source: USDA Economic Research Service (Per capita consumption of HFCS in the US from 1970 to 2016, in pounds). Health expenditures (HealthData.gov/U.S. Chronic Disease Indicators – CDI). Health Expenditures (Tracker Peterson Kaiser-health system tracker). The data is compiled by the authors and can be quoted with reference to it.

The results of the correlation analysis were also supportive of the current findings.

		Per capita chronic health expenditures
Per capita consumption of HFCS	r	.620**
	p	.000
	N	47

There was a significant positive correlation of 62 % between per capita HFCS consumption and per capita chronic health expenditures ($r = 0.620$, $p < 0.001$). It can be seen that, when per capita HFCS consumption increased by one unit, per capita health spending increased by 0.62 units. The display with the help of the scatterplot is as follows (Graph 3):

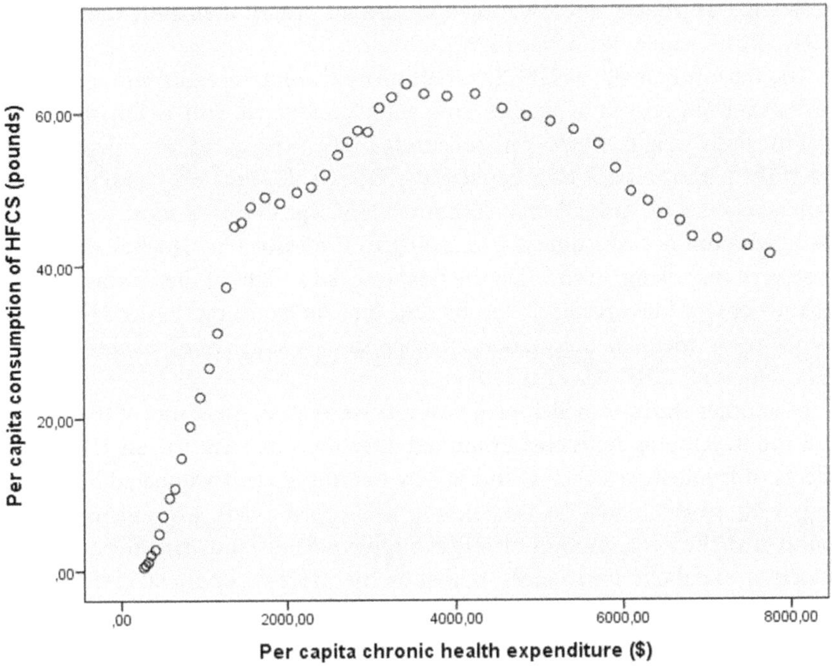

Graph 3: HFCS consumption and chronic health expenditures in the US

As one of the largest industries in the US, healthcare is steadily growing to meet the needs of an increasing population with an increasing life expectancy. The increase in chronic health expenditures in this growth is noteworthy (PAHO, 2001). Around 117 million adults in the US are struggling with chronic health problems. Seven out of 10 of the deaths in recent years were due to chronic diseases. (i) Lung and heart diseases, (ii) cancer, (iii) hypertension, (iv) Alzheimer's, and (v) diabetes and obesity stand out as the most common chronic diseases in the US. The two most important are heart disease and cancer, which account for almost 46 % of death cases. Three-quarters of the country's health expenditures are spent on chronic diseases. The annual cost of total cardiovascular disease is more than $400 billion. Cancer care costs are more than $200 billion, and the annual cost of diabetes is $245 billion. Obesity is a serious health problem in the US with more than 94 million people categorized as obese. The cost of obesity-related medical costs exceeds $180 billion annually. This leads to additional costs in terms of labor economics. Economy productivity is decreasing as people are allocating a significant part of their time to treatment (CDC, 2017; Fahey, 2017; Napalkov, 2009).

The harmful effects of HFCS, which turns chronic diseases into epidemics, have also been proven by studies. In a study conducted with rats, it was found that the body weight of male rats consuming HFCS increased more than the rats given the same amount of sugared water. The same situation was observed in female rats as well. Animals that consumed HFCS gained 48 % more weight than those who did not consume it. According to Professor Bart Hoebel, the results were very surprising. Even when the rats were fed a high-fat diet, it was not possible to observe this result. It can be said that the consumption of HFCS may contribute to the incidence of obesity when these results are adapted to humans (Bocarsly et al., 2010; Ma et al., 2014).

In another study, in which pregnant rats were used, the status of the mother and the developing fetus was examined after the rats were fed on HFCS. The effects of fructose, which is found widely in fruit juices, carbonated beverages, and ready-to-eat foods, on the embryo and fetuses were investigated. It was found that the consumption of HFCS-supplemented foods negatively affected maternal metabolic parameters as well as the placenta and fetal development in the pregnancy period. The risk of postnatal illness was also found to increase (Ardebili, 2015).

In another study, the brains of HFCS-consuming rats showed signs of slowing down. The memories and learning abilities of the rats were found to diminish. In the long term, consuming HFCS negatively affected the ability of the brain to acquire and remember information (Agrawal & Pinilla, 2012). According to Goldman (2009), the mercury used in the creation of HFCS is a dangerous material. Even low-dose microgram exposures in the womb were found to damage the brains of unborn children (Opalinski, 2012).

Many studies to date have shown that the consumption of unnatural sugar can cause pancreatic cancer. In a study conducted by the Nurses' Health Study in the US, during an 18-year follow-up, out of the 88,802 women that participated, 180 people were found to have pancreatic cancer. According to this study, tea sugar (sucrose) was not found to be associated with pancreatic cancer. However, corn syrup-rich diets significantly increased the likelihood of pancreatic cancer in a statistically significant manner. In the study titled Multiethnic Cohort, 434 out of 162,000 subjects who were followed for eight years were found to have pancreatic cancer. As a result of the analysis, abundant amounts of fructose in HFCS were found to cause pancreatic cancer. Researchers at the University of California, Los Angeles found that fructose accelerated the proliferation of cancer cells. In a study conducted on pancreas cell tumors, it was seen that fructose was used as an energy source by cancer cells and caused pancreatic cancer by disturbing glucose metabolism (Bulut, 2017; Michaud et al., 2002).

In another study, a drink containing glucose-fructose was given to healthy subjects and patients with pancreatic cancer. As a result, the fructose concentration, which was 1.9+/−0.4 mM in the healthy volunteers before drinking, increased to 16.3+/−1.2 mM in only 15 minutes. Fructose levels were also significantly higher in the volunteers with pancreatic cancer compared to the others (5.7+/−2.5 mM). This suggests that glucose-fructose intake may have a significant effect on many other diseases, including pancreatic cancer (Hui et al., 2009).

High fructose syrup (HFS) is mostly produced from corn. A significant proportion of sugar (fructose) in processed liquids and solid foods comes from corn, which is a genetically modified organism (GMO), just like the soybean plant. Corn is a plant that can easily become infected by harmful microorganisms such as bacteria, fungi, viruses, and parasites. Aflatoxin, a toxic fungus that can cause liver cancer, is common in corn. This is also the reason why HFCS is claimed to be responsible for digestive infections and various types of cancer (Erk, 2017).

HFCS consumption causes elevated blood cholesterol levels and blood clots. HFCS also inhibits the action of white blood cells, which protect the body against infections. In a study conducted on patients with renal insufficiency, the uric acid ratio in the blood of the patients who consumed corn syrup was extremely high. No such adverse effects were found in the subjects that were fed with the equivalent amount of glucose or lactose (milk sugar) (Karaca, 2017).

The introduction of HFCS in 1980, and sweeteners such as aspartame in 1991, along with the doubling of consumption of GMO products such as corn and soybeans, have created serious threats to human health, and have been a primary cause of the huge increase in chronic health expenditures in the US between 2000 and 2010. Studies conducted during the same period on this subject have shown that the number and quality of sperm in males dropped dramatically, and the risk of obesity and autism increased. The connection between low-quality sperm and the ratios of miscarriages support the findings related to HFCS damage (Dittmann, 2012).

Although there are a number of studies addressing the harms of HFCS in practice, there are also studies that claim that HFCS is not harmful, but a significant portion of these studies are supported by the US Corn Refiners Association. In addition, given that HFCS is made from genetically modified corn, the problems related to it are twice as bad. This can also explain how HFCS, a chemical substance, transforms chronic diseases into epidemics. Therefore, HFCS is a substance that needs to be vigorously avoided. As White puts it, experimental studies in the USA show that there is a significant causal relationship between glucose fructose (HFCS) consumption and chronic diseases (Esposito, 2016; White, 2013).

This result partly explains the explosion of chronic diseases in the US, where unprecedented levels of high blood pressure, obesity, diabetes (type II diabetes), and high cholesterol are observed. The US healthcare system is filled with health problems such as heart disease, stroke, kidney failure, gout, fatty liver, and reflux disease (Lyons, 2010). The role of sweeteners, especially HFCS consumption, is obvious in the increase of these problems. A product like HFCS, which was not available before 1970 in the US and whose usage increased 1,000 % over the last 30 years should be considered closely (BWI, 2007). These results need to be analyzed carefully in terms of public health. The new food technology which grew to meet the needs of a growing population is offering unhealthy food. This may lead to future problems that cannot even be imagined (Ackerman, 2002).

3.5. Discussion

Sugar regulations are different in every country. For instance, the EU has legislated limitations on the quantity of the HFCS produced. Japan has also put quotas on HFCS production to protect the market share of sugar. However, in the US, current sugar policies are supported by HFCS producers because they benefit from high sugar prices (Bennett, 2010; Mitchell, 2005). HFCS is prohibited in France, the Netherlands, Austria, Ireland, Sweden, Greece, Portugal, Slovenia, Denmark, and the United Kingdom. The US dropped their 10 % quota to 8 %, while Turkey increased its quota from 10 % to 15 %. In Turkey, the government increased the starch-based sugar quota to 312,500 tons, compared to 56,000 tons in Germany, 53,000 tons in Spain, and 32,000 tons in Italy. Starch-based sugar consumption per capita in Europe is one kilogram, while in Turkey it is around six kilograms (Niemi, 2003; Yalçın, 2017).

The need for sugar in the world and in Turkey increases daily. Today, the Turkish sugar market is under pressure from powers including the International Monetary Fund (IMF), the World Bank (WB) and multinational corporations (MNC). These powers actualize the policies they want in target countries through local politicians. Governments make laws and make bureaucracy arrangements, and interest groups share rents. The Sugar Institute, a regulatory and supervisory authority founded in Turkey in 2001, is a clear example of this situation. The objective of this authority is to meet the domestic sugar demand in Turkey with domestic production. In addition, it aims to increase exportation and maintain price stability in sugar production. However, the price of sugar has become even more expensive with the establishment of this regulatory authority. Turkey became familiar with concepts including sugar importing, illegal sugar, HFCS production, and HFCS imports, which it had not experienced before (Draycott, 2007; Kaymakçı, 2018).

The share of HFCS in total sugar production is expressed as a quota. The EU lifted its limits on sugar production and exports as of 1 October 2017, ending sugar quotas. European sugar producers can produce and export without restriction. Isoglucose production, however, seems to significantly increase market share in Europe, taking the place of sucrose, or sugar (Bache et al., 2014; European Commission, 2017).

Isoglucose. according to EU law, is glucose fructose syrup or high fructose corn syrup. The European starch industry is expected to increase the production of isoglucose to above the current production level of 676,000 tons. It is estimated that the production of isoglucose will reach 915,000 tons in 2028, due to market demand (Figure 9). Intensive demands from food and beverage manufacturers (soft drinks, ice cream, etc.) are particularly significant in this increase (Starch-Europe, 2017; Statista, 2020).

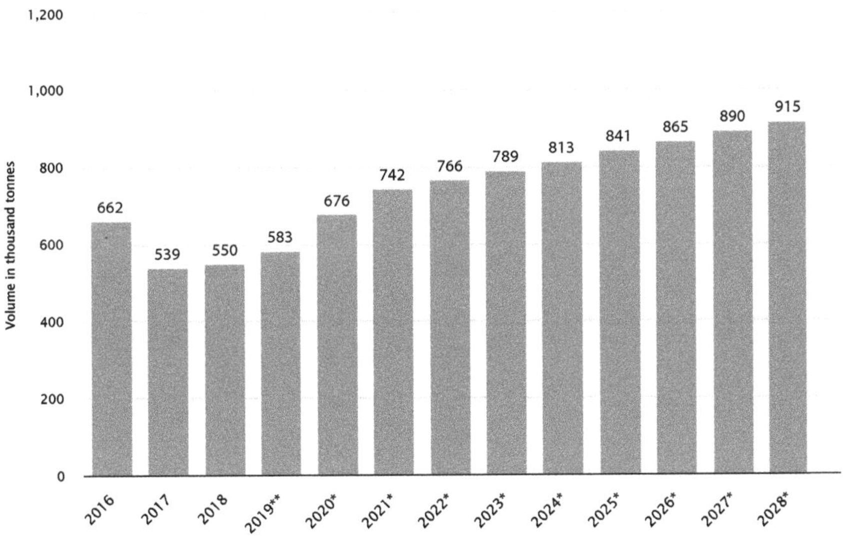

Figure 9: Forecast volume of high fructose corn syrup produced in the European Union (EU 27) from 2016 to 2028

Source: Statista, 2020.

The European Commission stated that it is tracking the consequences of abolishing quotas in the sugar and sweetener markets. Scientific evidence and policies are also being comprehensively investigated in terms of the possibility that high fructose causes excessive weight, obesity, and other health problems. The Commission has started to work towards this aim. In this process, it is necessary for all ingredients to be clearly stated on the labels of foodstuffs. The aim in requiring this is that consumers gain correct information about sugar content (European Parliament, 2017).

When statements are evaluated in terms of political economy, the concepts of efficiency and productivity emerge in the literature. The main objective of the economy is to provide efficiency. Efficiency is doing the right job – in this case, producing sugar. Productivity, on the other hand, is doing the job correctly – in other words, carrying out production at the lowest cost. However, the concept of productivity does not include efficiency. What is important in productivity is low cost and high profits. HFCS production implies this. Health problems that may arise due to the consumption of HFCS may lead to a significant burden on the economy in the coming periods.

Furthermore, the third-best policies make it possible to better understand the HFCS problem. The third-best policy depends on the amount of information available. It reveals the difference between a lack of information and a scarcity of information. It deals with situations where certainty is missing. Thus, the third-best policies are combined with the first- and second-best policies (Nar, 2020).

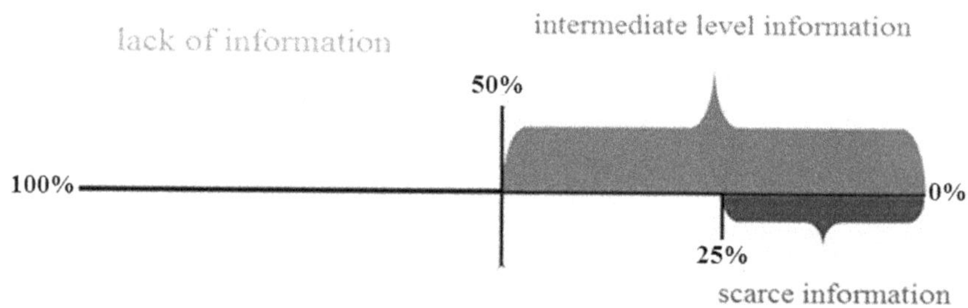

Figure 10: Third-Best Policy

Source: Nar, 2020. The third-best policy is a combination of first- and second-best policies. It reveals the difference between a lack of information and a scarcity of information.

According to the theory put forward by McGuire (1975), information is neither complete (100 %), as in the first-best policy-market economy, nor is it scarce (25 %), as in the second-best policy-public economy. The economy has an average information level (0–50 %). Nevertheless, the information is raw and not compiled. The average information level provides information about the rest of the economy. When the issue of risks and probability estimates are added, the economy reaches efficiency (Figure 10). Thus, the third-best policy combines the first- and second-best policies. When not enough information is known about the rest of the economy, it is possible not to tax sugar and ignore externalities, including the tax loss of the government. This theory shows that the analysis based on the third-best of the rest of the economy may actually be useful.

The debate in the United States over whether HFCS may be unhealthy and harmful or not remains fierce. One of the main reasons for the decline in production today is that people are becoming more aware and reducing their consumption, because what exactly this substance is remains an unknown issue. In the European Union countries, HFCS is expected to play a larger role in the market in the coming period. The EU Commission has started to examine its effects on health, and these studies are still ongoing. Therefore, since there is not enough information about corn syrup and sweeteners, actions such as not imposing taxes on sugar, the supporting of sugar agriculture, the subsidizing of it, and the providing of cheap credit will be extremely useful in terms of the rest of the economy. In this way, tax and similar losses suffered by the government will be much less than the health costs that HFCS is expected to cause. Under the high-profit margin, the emergence of human costs will also be avoided.

The concept of public benefit has led to the birth of public regulatory authorities, but these institutions have come to be overrun by corruption and irregularity with their numerous laws. However, regulations must be prepared in accordance with the legislation and requirements of social, economic, and commercial life. The supervision of these institutions should be transparent. The relationship between the government and the regulator should be clearly defined. It is important to strengthen civil society organizations and the independent media for this purpose, since most of the social facts are obtained from the media first-hand, as stated by McChesney. Nonetheless, capitalist media communication systems are dominated by a handful of corporations and global oligarchs. The media should be protected from political supervision, and instead supervised by professional organizations, and not allowed to engage in activities other than their primary activities, such as trade, construction, energy, etc.

This study of US sugar markets reveals that the US Department of Agriculture prefers to prioritize the interest of a handful of minorities instead of the public interest. This confirms the above findings and opens the way for the wide use of the HFCS substance in economies. The regulations in this area in the EU are carried out by the European Commission. By October 2017, various EU countries banned the production of HFCS, while others restricted it with quotas. However, it is clear that other EU countries will not be able to resist such a profitable item in the future. In Turkey, when the relevant regulatory authority became operational, sugar production first decreased, and then a boom in HFCS production and imports was experienced.

According to Dr. Mark Hymana, director of the Cleveland Clinic Medical Center in the US and one of the many doctors who opposes HFCS, this syrup contains fat, salt, chemicals, mercury, and dangerous and very low-quality food. It should definitely be avoided. However, the Corn Refiners Association has already targeted 700,000 medical doctors regarding the safety of the product. The US food industry accounts for 17 % of the economy; in fact, this sector is so profitable that millions of dollars are spent on convincing consumers and healthcare professionals of the benefits of this product.

In order to hide the truth, HFCS may be released to the market under misleading labels, such as natural sugar, corn sugar, corn syrup, inulin, starch-based sugar, isoglucose, dahlia syrup, tapioca syrup, glucose syrup, crystalline fructose, agave syrup, and even fruit fructose. By doing so, the aim is to conceal the reality of HFCS – which in fact leads to chronic diseases such as type 2 diabetes, heart disease, metabolic syndrome, osteoporosis, and cancer – and turn the negative perception in society into a positive one (Wellness Tips, 2007). In addition, the production process of this material is also unknown. Just like Pepsi and Coca-Cola products, production details are kept confidential. HFCS producers have defended the use of mercury in the production process, interestingly stating that it is not harmful. Expressions such as "the fish we eat may also contain mercury" are meaningless in such situations. Extreme profit has also blinded the eyes of the industry. Giving weight to sugar cultivation is important for creating healthy and sustainable generations. On this point, it is also important for consumers to choose more expensive sugar-based products instead of cheaper HFCS products that leave a bitter taste on the palate. Since it is not possible to eliminate the production of HFCS, the production of these substances should be limited to a minimum level. In addition, pregnant women, children, and people with health issues should be prevented from consuming this substance. In terms of this substance, which is said to have turned chronic diseases into epidemics, the economic benefits should be weighed against the social costs.

Global

Political

Economy

Chapter III International Political Economy

Political economy, rooted in moral philosophy, has been a normative field of study from the very beginning. Economics, on the other hand, strives to be independent of value judgments. With the influence of Marshall, the attempt was made to create a branch of science similar to mathematics and physics. With the publication in 1947 of the book *Foundations of Economic Analysis* by Paul Samuelson, who brought complex mathematical tools to the economy, the process of dividing political economy and economics into two separate fields was completed. The mainstream political economy eventually became the science of economics.

Global political economy, or international political economy, is an integral part of the science of political economy. It includes approaches that reveal the international leg of political economy, along with all of the methods that deal with international relations from an economic-political approach. It is the field of science that explains the distribution of wealth and power based on political and economic factors, and the complex interactions between them. It comprises applications that analyze economy, politics, and international relations together. The most distinctive feature of this new approach is that it evaluates international relations in terms of politics and economic relations. For example, the effects of taxes should be interpreted in one way in terms of economic science, and in another way in terms of political-economic science. Effects of taxes in terms of economics; monopoly can be evaluated in terms of its effects on oligopoly markets, household income level, saving and consumption behavior, or general market structures. In terms of international political economy, taxes (for example, customs duties) require evaluation not only in terms of their contribution to the national economy, but also in terms of international bilateral relations. Although the authority to impose and remove taxes belongs to individual states, high or low customs duties may create problems in terms of international relations, due to the fact that taxes have consequences in terms of economic as well as international relations, and these results directly affect political relations between countries. Similarly, the fact that a country has the status of most favored nation in terms of taxation not only increases the investments in the relevant countries, but also facilitates the mutual cross-border crossing of the citizens of the relevant countries. Hence, it should not be forgotten that economic arguments will have political consequences. This shows us that what appears as politics in international relations is actually nothing but political economy or mutual interest (Balaam & Veseth, 2004; Veseth & Balaam, 2020).

1. An Overview of International Political Economy

Today, political, social, and economic life is greatly affected by external factors. This situation causes economic, political, and social relations to become increasingly global (Jakob, 2009). The concept of the international political economy is also accepted as part of the new global division of labor (Heron, 2012).

There are three contemporary theories explaining the emergence, diffusion, and functioning of international political economy. The first is the two-sided theory of economy, stemming from economic liberalism. According to this theory, the development of markets leads to welfare maximization and increased productivity. The second theory is the approach influenced by Marxism and defined as the modern world system. According to this theory, the world market is based on the opposition and struggle between underdeveloped countries and developed capitalist economies. It takes as its point of departure the existence of an order based on economic exploitation. The third is the hegemonic theory of stability, which is associated with political realism. The theory of hegemonic stability links the rise and progress of the modern international economy to the liberal dominant powers. When viewed together, these three theories represent separate perspectives on the subject, but complement each other, and constitute important approaches in terms of the functioning of international political economy (IPE). The first theory of international political economy focuses on the evolution of the world economy, the movement of economic activities from one country or region to another. The second explains the rising and declining economic systems. And the third highlights the increasing integration processes of national economies, the increasing influence of foreign powers on local interests, and the increasing importance of globalization in this process (Gilpin, 2001).

What we call international political economy is essentially the sum of international economy and international relations (Jackson et al., 2019). In other words, it is the field of science that explains the processes of globalizing capitalism and the complex political processes and struggles that emerge from it. Figure 11 shows the formation process of the international political economy. Accordingly, on the left side of the figure is shown the international economic area – in other words, the economic region where states interact with each other. On the right side of the figure is shown the formation process of national policies and the actors involved in this process. The actors involved in the political process are listed as (i) voters, (ii) politicians, (iii) bureaucrats, and (iv) interest groups, according to the Virginia Political School. It is emphasized that political decisions emerge as a result of the common interactions of these groups. Another factor in the formation of national policies is the decisive role of institutions in the process, since institutions are the basic policy tool that enables individuals and groups to maximize their benefits economically. The shaded area, representing the intersection set, explains the international political economy (IPE). International political economy, from an interdisciplinary perspective, focuses on how the global economy affects national policies, while at the same time evaluating the effects of national policies on the global economy. It demonstrates that international relations are not independent of the international economy, and explores how resource allocation occurs in different economic systems (CFI, 2021; Nar, 2020; Rupert & Solomon, 2006).

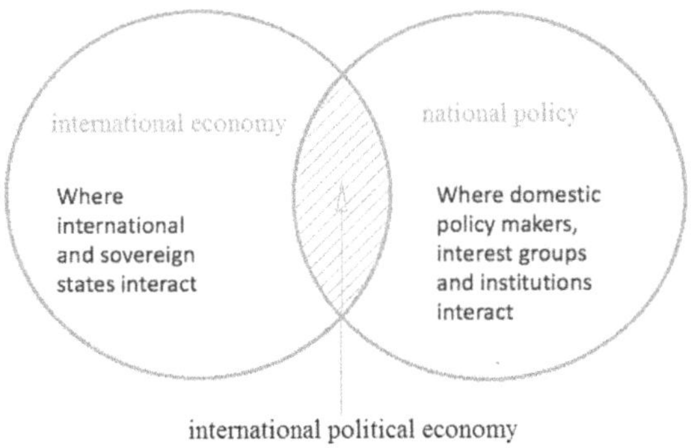

Figure 11: Representation of International Political Economy
Source: CFI, 2021

International political economy examines the two areas of international policy and international economy through different social systems and social groups. The main research areas of international political economics today are international migrant policies, problems related to economic globalization, research on international trade, problems arising from international finance, economic-political problems between rich and poor countries, and the role played by multinational corporations (MNC). In fact, one of the main areas of study of today's political economic approaches is economic globalization and the problems that MNCs have created in a hegemonic sense in the process. The harsh statements in the United Nations Economic and Social Council (ESOSOC) Subcommittee Report on this subject are extremely important. The report draws attention to the fact that the exploitative practices of transnational companies, which are part of globalization, in developing countries have reached significant dimensions. In fact, it is pointed out in the report that anti-hegemonic activities should be evaluated with a political economic approach. It is emphasized that the most basic areas where the costs of globalization are reflected are the areas of public expenditures and taxation (Gilpin, 2001; Enderwick, 2006; Veseth & Balaam, 2020).

1.1. Major Approaches in International Political Economy

In line with the explanations above, it is possible to define international political economy (IPE) as the interaction of political and economic factors at the global level. IPE covers many areas, from the everyday life of people to the relations of governments at the national and international level. Among the many fields of study of political economy are subjects such as trade, finance, public policies, environment, industry, foreign direct investments (FDI), and international aid. For example, a country's level of benefiting from global investment opportunities is mainly related to the degree of openness. The level of openness is, in turn, primarily a result of the political decisions of that country, and shows the effect of the policy on the economy. Similarly, the economic provisions determined by the political policies of the EU member countries also show the effects of the policy on the economy. It is also possible to talk about political economic approaches in encouraging labor migration with political decisions by governments that are trying to increase their votes. In other words, politics can permeate all areas of economic and social life. Again, international aid, as well, can have economic dimenions, but at the same time bring political dependency. Thus, economy and politics always go hand in hand, and we can say that the invisible hand of the market merges with the visible hand of politics, and the distinction between politics and economy can be seen to disappear.

In the evaluation of the international political economy, several different theoretical perspectives are used. These include: (i) mercantilist, (ii) liberal, and (iii) structuralist approaches. Mercantilists are associated with realists who argue that power, security, and independence are vital to the interests of nation-states. This approach associates power with the economy and argues that the power of the state is essentially as much as its wealth. Liberals have optimistic views on the ability of people and states to build peaceful relations and a new world order. This perspective draws attention to the importance of global markets, the necessity of free trade, and the presence of market forces in solving economic problems. It also focuses on limiting the role of states in the economy. The structuralist approach is based on Marxist or Neo-Marxist analyses, and explains how socially dominant powers serve the economic interests of the classes. Mercantilist, liberal, and structuralist approaches all focus on personal interests, national interests, and the interests arising from the functioning of the international system, and on the political economic solution to the problems associated with them.

The concept of contemporary international political economy emerged as a sub-branch of international relations during the period of competition between the Soviet Union and the United States during the Cold War period (1945–91). Along with economic factors, the causes and formation processes of international conflict, and the relations between them, have been discussed and developed. Although the analyses initially focused on international security, they subsequently came to address economic issues such as economic security, market actors, multinational company policies, international banks, cartels such as OPEC, and international organizations such as the IMF. International political economy gained more importance as a result of various international economic events, such as the collapse of the Bretton Woods international monetary system in 1971 and the 1973–74 oil crisis. Official political economy focuses mainly on the analysis of Marxist or liberal schools, and generally deals with two kinds of issues. The first issue that international political economy (IPE) focuses on is how policy constrains domestic economic choices. For example, the liberalization of trade in agricultural products in the EU may adversely affect countries exporting agricultural products. Or, sugar production quotas applied in EU countries for a period may impose restrictions on the economic income of the countries. The second issue that IPE focuses on is the restrictive role played by individuals, firms, and lobbying activities on the foreign policies of governments. In such cases, the political choices of governments also significantly limit their ability to make future decisions. For example, governments that strive to attract foreign investments to their country can reconsider their decisions towards foreign investors under pressure from lobbies. They even offers as many incentive tools as possible to foreign investors, including tax breaks. We thus see that in the modern world international relations operate in large part as the interaction between politics and economics (Andersson, 2020; Andersson et al., 2007; Art & Jervis, 1985; Mansfield, 2004; Veseth & Balaam, 2020).

2. Globalization and International Political Economy

One of the main reasons for the growth of the mutual interaction between economy and politics is globalization. Since 1850, the world population has increased by five times, per capita income by eight times, world income by 40 times, and world trade by 540 times. With globalization, attention was drawn to the nature of the economic and political processes that connect the markets. While globalization is for some considered a phenomenon of trade, international investment, technology transfer, and migration, for others it has been defined as a concept that directly affects public policies, including political, cultural, and information sharing, in addition to its economic dimension. However, the main emphasis is on the economic dimension of globalization. (Steger, 2017). The economic dimension of globalization is marked by competition among firms to secure increased profits by participating in international markets (Sugrue & Maher, 1993). Economic globalization has thus emerged with increased economic openness, integrating national economies and allowing for the free flow of capital and investment and the formation of transnational alliances; all of these features can then be said to make up the "**current international political economy**" (Carrion, 2010).

The concept of globalization today differs from other periods in three ways:

(i) The speed of international exchange: Due to the important developments in information, communication, computer, and micro- and nanotransaction technologies, international transaction costs have decreased and financial transactions are now possible with the touch of a computer key.
(ii) Integrated market structures: The level of global integration and cohesion of local and national market structures has increased more than ever before.
(iii) The role played by multinational companies in business life: The activities of multinational companies have become more important than in the past. While trade is globalizing, foreign direct investments have spread all over the world in a global network.

Two main features come to the fore in the globalization process. First, neoliberalism places less emphasis on the concepts of equality and justice. Second, in developing countries, neoliberalism seeks to use state mechanisms to reduce the role of the state. The following neoliberal policies emphasize the economic aspect of globalization (Steger, 2017):

1. Privatization of public enterprises and economic deregulation
2. Trade and industry liberalization
3. Massive tax cuts
4. Enforcement of policies aimed at controlling inflation through monetarist measures
5. Strict controls on organized labor
6. Reducing public expenditures, especially social expenditures

7. Restricting the coverage (size) of governments
8. Enforcement of policies for the expansion of international markets
9. Removal of controls on global financial flows

3. The Development of the Globalization Process

The existence of two major turning points in the development of the globalization process can be mentioned. The first turning point (Figure 12) appears partly as an economic and technological process, and partly as a political process. The 1940s is the second turning point of globalization and is known as the beginning of contemporary globalization.

Contemporary globalization is a concept that includes economic and technological as well as political, sociocultural and environmental developments. It is thus possible to define contemporary globalization as a supranational interaction in which transnational structures are established and the integration of economic, technological, political, sociocultural, and environmental processes at the global, regional, and local levels are encouraged. By another definition, globalization consists of the integration processes that lead to the economic, political, and cultural unification of the world. Globalization in the economic sphere means production, exchange, and commodity consumption. Politically, globalization encompasses practices related to the production and distribution of power in societies. Sociocultural globalization defines the worldwide cultural flows of social life. Globalization is harmful to some, because it differentiates people and alienates them. For some, it is useful because it allows interaction with Western popular culture as defined by centers such as New York, Hollywood, London, and Milan (Dreher et al., 2008; Nar, 2021).

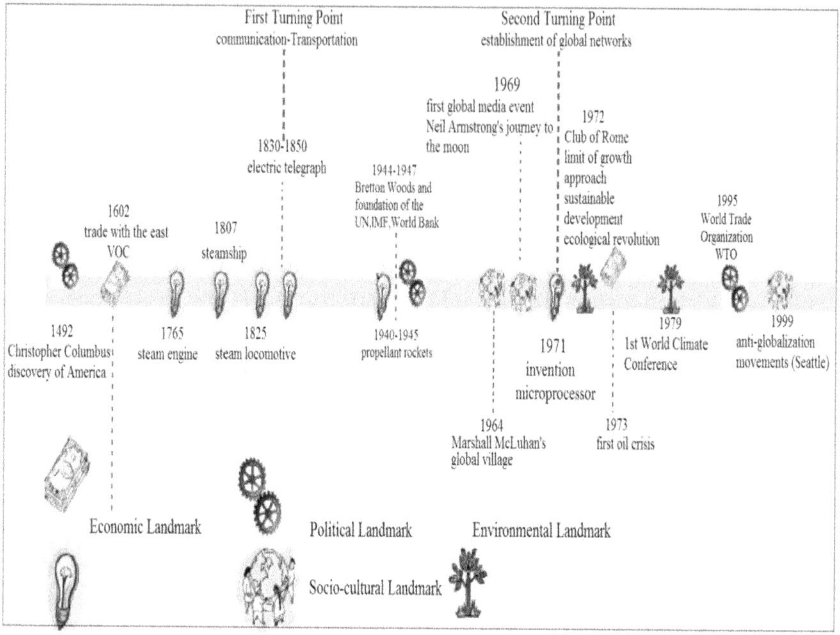

Figure 12: The development of the globalization process
Source: Dreher et al., 2008.

Canadian communication theorist Marshall McLuhan brought a new perspective to the understanding of globalization in 1964 with his concept of the global village. McLuhan argued that the use of communication tools will gradually increase and the world will consequently transform into an integrated village. Thus, the planet we live on will in a sense become smaller and easier to reach. An event taking place in any part of the world can be learned of by other people in different places instantaneously. Since the concepts of time and space lose their former significance, the work done and the distances covered will increase over time. However, globalization has not remained solely the product of the modernization process, capitalist ideology, or any particular event. It spreads its reach as a large organization covering many areas, including the political, economic, military, geographical, and cultural. At the global level, people have become more dependent on a wider network of others, not only technologically or scientifically, but also socioculturally, economically, and politically. While the world economy has differentiated and allowed the globalization of economies, the globalization of economies has also led to changes in policies and the removal of restrictions. This situation weakened the sovereign power of nation states and has almost eliminated their ability to set policies on their own (Das, 2006; Nar, 2015; UN, 2018; Thussu, 2006).

Changes and developments occurring especially after the end of the Cold War made it necessary for a new understanding to emerge in the world, in terms of economy, politics, and culture. In this emerging new order, it has become almost impossible for states to continue their existence isolated within their own borders. Globalization has forced the familiar state model of societies to change in line with its unique systematic structure. In this context, the differentiation of the world economy and the globalization of the economy caused the policies that shape world politics to change. This situation weakened the sovereign power of nation states, and did not allow them to implement policies on their own. Today, the globalization process can be seen as a new world order that makes economic relations between countries more dependent than before, a system in which worldwide economic goods and services are controlled by a few multinational companies, and trade is liberalized by crossing borders. Therefore, globalization not only makes countries and citizens dependent economically, but also affects societies politically and culturally, and makes them dependent on each other (Das, 2006; Keyman et al., 1998; Nar, 2015). It is understood that the most important change in this dependence is concentrated on the (1) consumption and (2) investment (production) activities of the countries.

4. Globalization of Consumption

The most obvious example that demonstrates the interdependence of economics and policies is the globalization of consumption. In this process, companies shape their investment policies in order to make consumption massive. While the understanding of short-term consumption is imposed on society in general, political policies also support this process. In this understanding, as a requirement of capitalism, people consume goods such as furniture, clothing, white goods, and cars, while attributing meanings to this consumption through symbolic values. Thus, individuals can satisfy their desires, such as being accepted in society and being happy (Bocock, 1993; Kellner, 2002). In this way, consumption culture generally prepares the environment for the formation of taste-based lifestyles and the development of selfish personality types (Featherstone, 2007). In this sense, the phenomenon of consumption corresponds to two types of understanding: (i) consumption is the understanding that is valid in all societies and explains the consumption tradition, style, and behavior of each society, and (ii) consumer culture is a process associated with postmodern societies as a result of the free market or liberal economy (Odabaşı, 2006).

Today, it is possible to say that the basic function of consumption has changed. For example, the telephone, which is used as a communication tool, is also evaluated through other meanings as an indicator of comfort and status. In this approach, consumption becomes an indicator of social codes, rather than merely meeting natural needs. Therefore, in this system, social values and classifications take the place of basic needs and pleasures. In other words, instead of meeting a rational need, consumers try to satisfy their status desires. In the consumer society, where the distinction between real needs and fake needs has disappeared, the individual believes that buying and displaying consumer goods is a sign of social privilege and prestige (Bocock, 1993; Fromm, 2017).

Globalization has expanded its sphere of influence on societies by increasing its share in worldwide consumption, especially in technological products. A limited number of multinational companies have become a power that starts with technological products, continues with other products, and can reach many parts of the world thanks to its broad market network. These companies have become representatives of an understanding that can guide not only the economy, but also the consumption, culture, ethnicity, boundaries, and, in sum, all decision-making mechanisms of societies in the process. In this context, in today's society, people are directed to consumption rather than production as a requirement of capitalism, and are referred to as a consumer society. In fact, it is the producers – that is, the capitalist owners of capital – who in most cases have the right to decide on many issues, such as the value that individuals ascribe to objects and which objects will be consumed. The sole purpose here is to consume, and to encourage more consumption than before. However, individuals are motivated to certain behaviors by their self-structure, which also provides satisfaction to the person. Accordingly, capitalism deceives every person with a new type of pleasure according to the conditions of the day, making the consumer willing to spend. Each product offered to the market triggers the feeling of pleasure in the person, and reveals the conditions that create a new economic need (Fromm, 2017).

In addition, it is a fact that globalization has created a new culture in terms of distinctive consumption. This culture is a mass consumption-oriented approach that compels everyone to be a consumer by creating a continuity of needs determined by certain power centers, which develops beyond the control of the individual or society. In principle, this perception of a new culture is what sees community members as consumers, not producers, and shapes them in that way.

It is a culture that gives all kinds of political incentives to societies to be consumers, and can put pressure on societies (Bauman, 1998).

This cultural understanding forces people to consume. As a requirement of this, the primary task of a person's social environment has become consumption, rather than production. In fact, practically the only indicator of economic development in many societies is consumption. At the least, such a perception has become entrenched in societies – so much so that many countries determine the results of a financial crisis or growth rates according to the objects consumed in the country and adjust their economic policies accordingly. Examples of this would include the number of houses, cars, or textiles sold, so that the basic measure is always the quantitative equivalent of what is consumed. This perception has turned people into machines that are ready for consumption both psychologically and physiologically. Globalization, then, has reinforced this process with the excess of product preference it offers. In this sense, consumption in today's society has turned into a culture of unlimited and insatiable need, having dispensed with the innocent idea of meeting the basic needs of people. According to the anthropologist Bronislaw Malinowski, the main function of culture should be to meet the basic needs of human beings, such as food, shelter, reproduction, psychological needs, and security. In other words, a cultural element continues to be maintained as long as it has a certain function in terms of meeting the needs of the individual. In this understanding, the habit of consumption, which is a cultural product, exists to meet the unlimited needs of people and should be continuous because it has a certain function (Bauman, 1998; Nar, 2015).

Today, people are no longer defined by what they produce, but by what they consume. In fact, it is mostly the producers – namely, multinational companies – who decide what to consume and what not to consume, or how much to consume. In addition to this, it is the multinational companies and the countries representing them that develop and market these products, benefiting greatly from this consumption in material and moral terms, rather than the consumers who are satisfied with these conditions. Individuals today are thus defined not by what they produce, but by what they consume (Ritzer, 2009). Making consumption economically advantageous with elements of popular culture then causes consumers to behave in similar ways. As a result of this, it is aimed to have a unity and convergence in the consumption values shared among people. People's lifestyles, preferences, behaviors, and habits are increasingly being reshaped by popular culture elements, which are an important server of globalization. It is possible to see the traces of globalization, especially its popular culture dimension, in many practices such as the movies watched, the music listened to, the food eaten, the clothes worn, the items used, the art admired, and even the behaviors of daily life. Global capitalists, especially by using the power of the media, impose the consumption behaviors of developed societies onto other societies and target audiences. It is thus intended that other societies show similar consumption behavior. In this context, the acceptance of popular culture elements as a guiding force in people's behavior by the masses and societies emerges as a clear indicator of political and cultural, as well as economic, globalization (Erkızan, 2002; Ritzer, 2009; Steger, 2017;Tomlinson, 1999; Veblen, 2014).

5. International Investments and Political Economy

International investments are cross-border investments made through capital and finance companies. Such investments can be either direct or indirect. Indirect investments generally refer to investments made abroad through investment instruments such as stocks or bonds. Such investments, which are described as portfolio investments, can be made by financial companies as well as other companies or individual portfolio investors. International direct investments, on the other hand, are the forms of direct involvement in production activities by a foreign investor through establishing a facility or purchasing mergers in order to produce in another country.

The role of financial markets in the realization of investments is extremely important. Financial markets basically fulfill three functions:

(i) organization of international payment through the foreign exchange market,
(ii) supply of stocks through the stock market, and
(iii) financing of investments through money and capital markets.

Figure 13, depicts the classification of the market structures. Accordingly, the capital markets consist of two types of elements: the primary and the secondary. The first element named as the primary market, consists of the money collection process of private or corporate organizations such as commercial companies, state organizations or nongovernmental organizations (NGOs). In other words, the primary market consists of securities issued by private or legal institutions and markets where account owners realize first-hand procurement. The secondary market consists of buying and selling of shares, bonds, and securities between investors after the initial sale (Williams, 2011).

Until the 1970s, financial markets were national markets and were politically regulated by the Bretton Woods system. There was a fixed exchange rate in this system based on foreign exchange and capital controls. The US dollar was the leading foreign currency. During this period, the world economy also showed a solid growth. After the system was abandoned in 1973, a radical transformation was experienced in the world economy, and the fixed exchange rate was replaced by the free exchange rate. Controls on capital movements have been largely abolished, and capital has become the most active element. The relationship between the real economy and the financial system has been abandoned. Financial markets have dominated the rest of the economy (Kohonen, 2009).

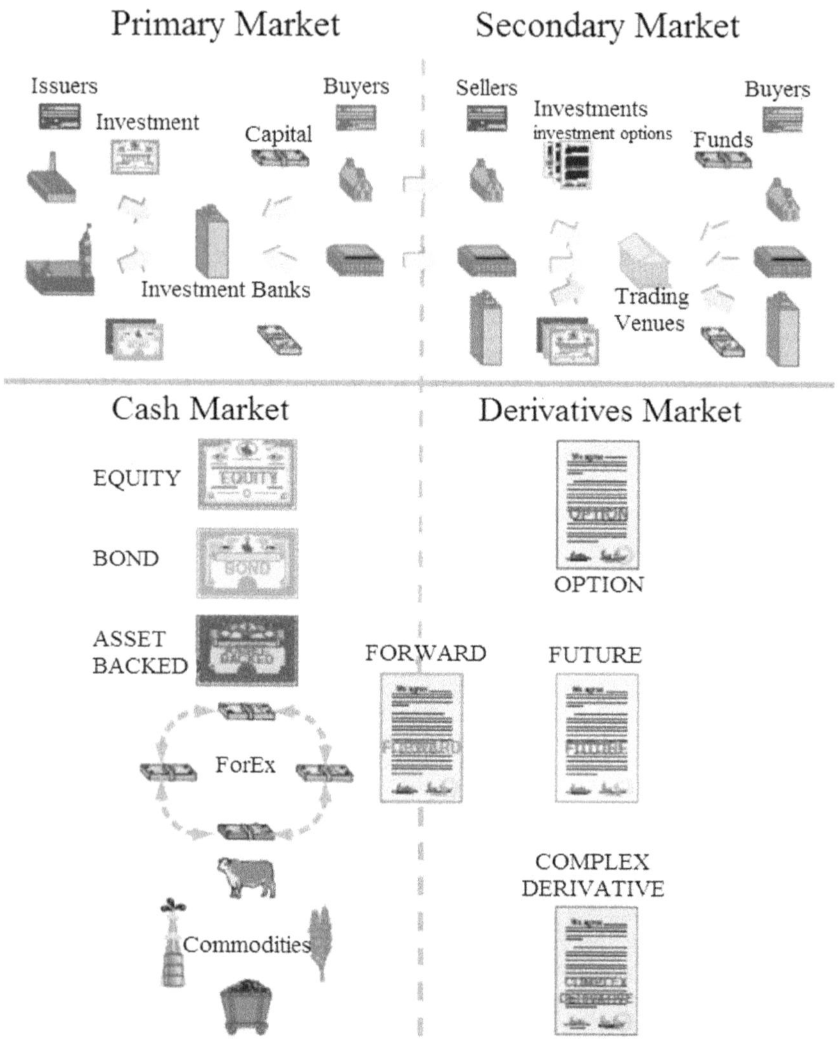

Figure 13: Taxonomy of markets

Source: (Williams, 2011) . Figure 13. Marketssegment into primary versus secondary and cash versus derivative to highlight different aspects of their purpose.

This situation, which we can refer to as financial globalization, involves the integration of all financial markets in the world into a single international financial market. The main reasons underlying the integration of financial markets are the liberalization of financial activities, technological development, and the increase in institutionalization. Governments have liberalized their relevant laws in line with the demands of the markets, in order to attract international investments to their countries. While technological developments connect the markets to each other with computer networks, efficiency in global markets has increased. It has also been possible for investors in far corners of the world to access information and prices in the market in real time. At the same time, institutional investors – pension funds, insurance funds, investment companies, savings funds, and even commercial banks – have begun to replace individual investors in the market. These factors have led to the consolidation of markets and the acceleration of globalization. In the 1980s, countries with higher risks and uncertainties were defined as emerging markets, compared to developed markets. Since risk and uncertainty are high in developing countries, the expected return is also high. For this reason, emerging market economies still continue to offer attractive profit opportunities to institutional investors of developed countries. The globalization of financial markets, meanwhile, leads to the emergence of new derivative investment instruments (Kocaman, 2003; Stiegler, 2010).

5.1. Total Portfolio Investments in the World

Investments in financial instruments and derivatives such as stocks, bonds, interest, and exchange rates are the leading financial investment instruments. Such investments are speculative investments and are referred to as portfolio investments. Portfolio investments have the ability to quickly leave the country in which they are based, at the touch of a computer key, due to their mobile nature. This situation leads to great risks, unpredictable uncertainties, global crises, and negative effects on global welfare. However, the size of financial markets today proves that the most important pillar of globalization is financial markets. In the evaluation of portfolio investments, net investments are calculated by taking the difference between assets and liabilities. Accordingly, capital investments made by non-residents in a country constitute liabilities, while investments abroad by residents (as well as the reserves they evaluate in foreign markets) represent assets. The difference gives the international net portfolio investment amount. In portfolio investments, the deficit of the net investment position means that the liabilities are more than the assets, while in the opposite case, the investment surplus is mentioned.

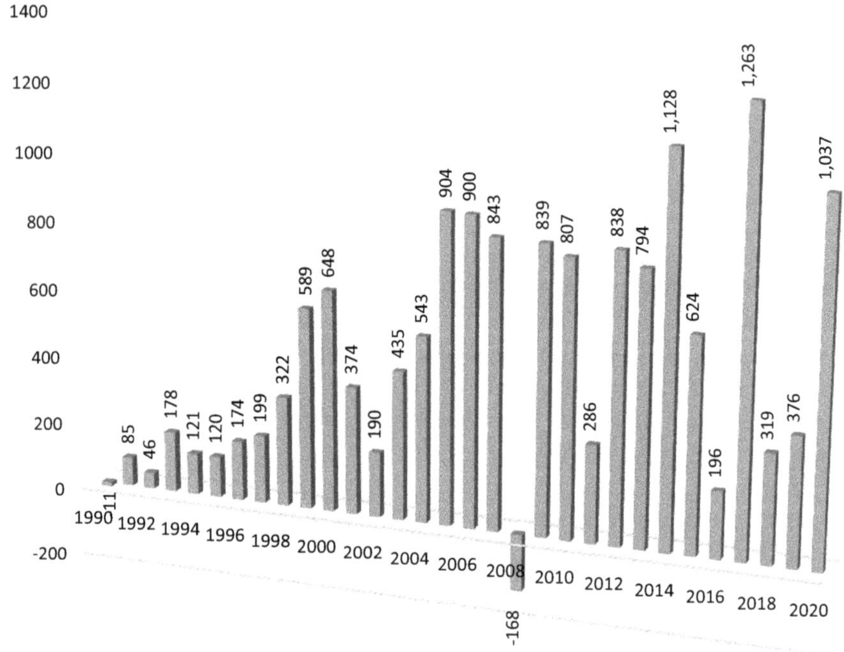

Graph 4: Net portfolio investments in the world 1990–2020 ($)
Source: (Knoema, 2022; World Bank, 2022a).

In Graph 4, net portfolio investments around the world are analyzed. In 1990 and 2008, the net portfolio investments followed a negative course with the effect of global crises and were realized as −11 billion dollars and −168 billion dollars. World net portfolio investments, which reached the level of 1.1 trillion dollars in 2014, continued to increase between 1971–2020, despite the fact that they have fluctuated significantly in recent years.

Total portfolio investments in the world were 12 trillion dollars in 2001. In 2021, it reached a significant 76 trillion dollars. It can be said that portfolio investments vary depending on the global conjuncture and economic fluctuations (Graph 5).

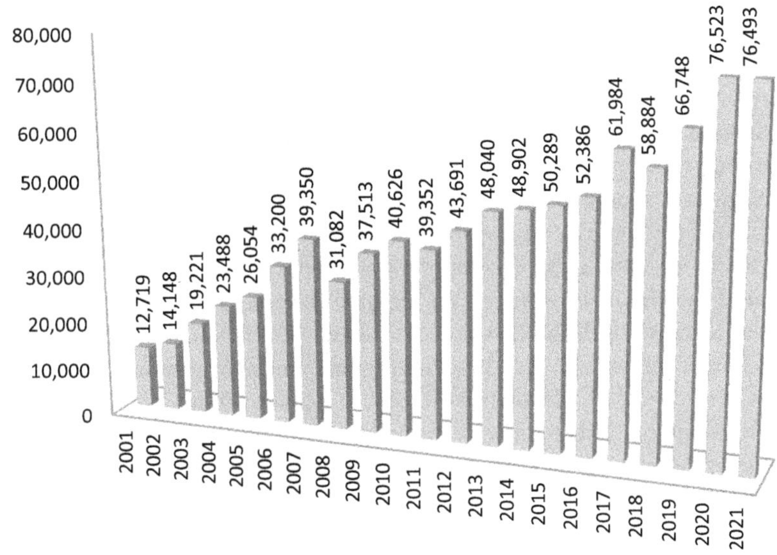

Graph 5: Total portfolio investments in the world 2001–2021 ($)
Source: (IMF, 2022a)

As of 2022 data, the Netherlands ranks first in world portfolio investments. Other countries in the top five are listed as Italy, Spain, Hong Kong, and Germany, respectively. The data revealed the superiority of the European region in terms of portfolio investments (Knoema, 2022). However, major disruptions have occurred in cross-border portfolio flows due to the COVID-19 crisis. In this situation, investments came to a standstill in many emerging markets as well as in some developed economies. While many countries made sudden stops in their portfolio investments due to the effect of the global epidemic, it was understood that bank inflows compensated for the decreases in the portfolio flows in this process to varying extents. In addition, it is understood that there have been unprecedented capital outflows from emerging market economies due to the fact that foreign investors preferred to sell their portfolio assets due to the COVID-19 epidemic. Considering the scale and speed of capital outflows in the current crisis, it is about four times larger than the 2008 financial crisis. As of 2021, although the outlook remains fragile and global uncertainties continue to put pressure on global investors, signs of stability continue to come (IMF, 2022b).

5.2. Worldwide Direct Investments

While the economic field where globalization is most prominent is the field of international finance, the second popular field of globalization is foreign direct investments. Political, economic, and technological developments constitute the driving force behind globalization. With the end of the Cold War, the process of globalization gained intense momentum. In addition to greatly reduced travel costs, the increase in the speed and quality of transportation, as well as innovations in the fields of computers and telecommunication, significantly increased the size of investments in the global arena. This situation has led to a global increase in direct investments offered by MNCs. Especially since the mid-1980s, it can be seen that direct investments made by multinational companies have reached a significant level. Today, foreign direct investments are mostly made by industrialized countries, especially by American and Western European companies. Most of these investments are in the services sector. Investments in advanced technology sectors mostly cover automotive and information technologies (Gilpin, 2001). Implementations such as advantages in energy, government guarantees, price guarantees, raw material, and labor costs, legal advantages, product purchase guarantees, protection of intellectual property rights, guarantees against nationalization, and free profit transfer are important in accelerating foreign direct investment inflows. All such arrangements are the effects of political decisions on the global economy. In addition, tax advantages (tax discounts, low corporate tax, zero tax, etc.) are extremely effective. For example, Ireland, which was one of the poorest countries in Europe in the 1980s, became one of the countries with the highest growth rate in Europe in 2004 with the low tax rates it applied to foreign investors (Giray, 2016; Reinsdorf and Slaughter, 2009; Rudra, 2008).

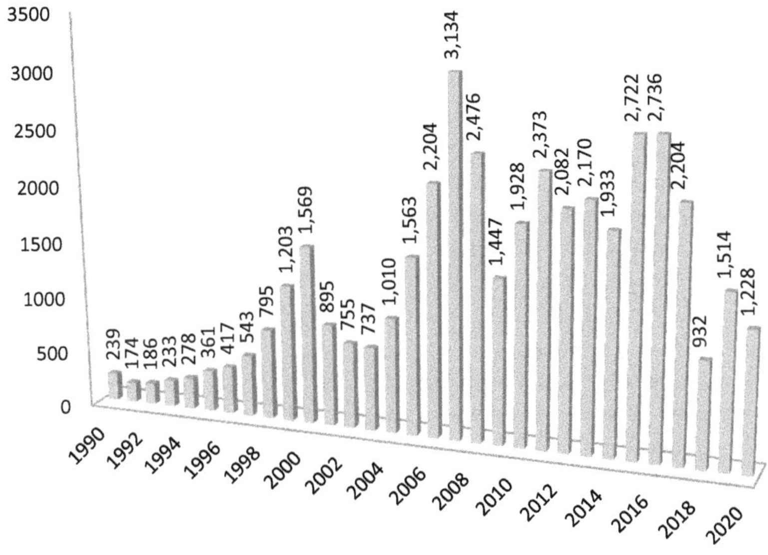

Graph 6: Worldwide direct investments 1990–2020 ($)
Source: (World Bank, 2022b)

Graph 6 shows worldwide direct investments. Accordingly, foreign direct investments (FDI) grew rapidly after the 1990s. Most of these investments have been made to OECD member countries and developing countries, especially Asian countries. While there are various ways of classifying direct investments, a simple classification system is in terms of vertical and horizontal direct investments. Accordingly, horizontal direct investments are known as market seeking, meaning that the multinational company produces the same goods and services in the target country that it produces in its own country. Vertical investing, on the other hand, is known as resource seeking. Geographically, it is defined as shifting production activities to countries where production factors are cheap and abundant (Baldwin & Winters, 2004; Bishop, 2004; Mishkin, 2006).

As a result of the rapid transformation in technology, the duration of time is shortened, significant savings are made from the freeing of time, and international commercial costs are rapidly reduced. The market and resource searches of developed countries are increasing in parallel with these developments. US-led industrialized countries strive to reduce trade and investment barriers as much as possible. The attempt to remove trade barriers between countries was made with the General Agreement on Tariffs and Trade (GATT). In addition, countries are encouraged to turn to more deregulation and privatization practices. This situation leads to an increase in direct investments around the world. As a result of these and similar developments, FDI inflows, which were 239 billion dollars in 1990, reached 3 trillion dollars in 2007.

After the global crisis observed in 2008, the decrease in foreign direct investments (FDI) continued in 2009 as well. The decline of 250 billion dollars in acquisitions and mergers worldwide in 2009 was one of the most important reasons for this contraction. In 2010, on the other hand, an increasing trend was observed in global investments, albeit on a small scale. In this period, it can be said that risks and uncertainties stemming from global fragility eased, albeit partially. The decline observed in investments in 2018 is mainly considered as a reflection of negative situations such as global fluctuations, falling profitability rates, financial pressure, shrinkage in credits, and slowdown in tax cuts.

With the effect of the COVID-19 global epidemic, foreign direct investments decreased by 18 % in 2020 compared to the previous year and decreased to 1.2 trillion dollars. In this regression, first of all, it was important to close the border gates to human crossings in order to prevent human mobility, and stop all domestic and international land, air, and railway flights, except for the permitted ones. In addition, the suspension of all economic activities in terms of production, investment, tourism, and trade has been decisive. Therefore, in 2020, there was a contraction of –3.1 % worldwide. After expanding by 5.9 % in 2021, global growth is expected to slow to 4.4 % in 2022 and then slow to 3.8 % in 2023. Increasing energy prices and supply disruptions have caused higher and broader-based inflation than expected in developed economies and emerging market economies, especially in the USA. The ongoing contraction in China's real estate sector and the slower-than-expected recovery in private consumption have revealed limited growth prospects. In parallel with these developments, direct investments affected by economic contractions continue to be a long-term source of concern for policy makers. In developing countries where international investments are indispensable, FDIs are seen as essential for sustainable industrial development, which makes it necessary for the global investment environment to include more transparent, non-discriminatory, and encouraging policies in today's conditions (IMF, 2022b; World Bank, 2022b).

The countries that attract the most FDI are, in order, the USA, China, France, and Germany. In the ranking of the countries offering the most FDI, the USA, France, and Japan come first. Besides, while the shares of developed regions from foreign direct investments are decreasing, the shares of developing regions from direct investments are increasing (UNCTAD, 2020).

Governments, which constitute the political pillar of this process, remove the restrictions on financial institutions and encourage globalization by allowing the free movement of capital. Borrowers can borrow on more favorable terms, while investors can turn to overseas investments. While globalization affects international relations and national economies, international political economy also emerges as a reality. In the process of globalization, politics and power relations become more differentiated, and come to direct international politics and economic policies (Pelaez & Pelaez, 2008). In this respect, international political economy has a wide range of fields of study, such as globalization, global market structures, international trade, international investments, international commercial agreements, international financial markets, global financial crises, political risk and uncertainties, development economics, cross-border economic problems, and consumption culture. In this sense, international political economy is defined as "a new discipline that analyzes the formation of economic and political power balances around the world" (Paquin, 2019).

Political Economy of International Arbitration

Chapter IV Political Economy of International Arbitration

Globalization brings technological advances, significant reductions in transportation and transmission costs, and easier integration of national markets with international markets. The free movement of labor, goods, capital, and service mobility on a global scale thereby becomes possible. With globalization, tariff and non-tariff barriers between countries are removed, restrictions on trade are eased, and economic interaction between countries increases. Parallel to all these developments, it is seen that foreign direct and indirect investments have reached significant rates (OECD, 2011). The political economy of international arbitration is a reflection of policy attempts to get a larger share of the global economy. In other words, it is the whole of the efforts of politicians to harmonize national law with global law, for economic reasons such as international investments. Concepts such as international law, international investments, globalization, and multinational corporate activities are the main areas of investigation in the political economy of international arbitration.

1. The Political Economy of International Arbitration

Attempts to get a larger share from the global economy directly affect national politics and put pressure on governments. Structural problems within countries, especially in the economic sense, make it almost mandatory for governments to engage in international interaction. In parallel with the increasing degrees of economic openness, the level of economic globalization of countries is also increasing. With free movement, global capital and investment flows are increasing, transnational business alliances and mergers are increasing, and FDIs are becoming a global power. Such formations appear as a part of the new world order, and constitute one of the main areas of study of international political economy. Especially since the 1970s, many host countries have adopted differently designed policies to attract FDI to their countries. Governments are influenced by the political power and dominance of foreign companies, and often make decisions according to their wishes. Therefore, in practice, perceptions are widespread that multinational companies drive production, reduce their tax revenues, lower labor environment and other regulatory standards, and bring negativity with them as well as their contribution to the country's economies. However, despite negative judgments, it is a fact that the number of bilateral and regional agreements and legal regulations that encourage greater liberalization and protection of international investment has increased in recent years. International lobbies prefer such agreements and legal arrangements to provide greater bargaining power, and can direct countries receiving investments. Companies that have no other purpose than profitability, though, determine their investment policies with the understanding of mass consumption (toxic consumption) and short-term consumption. The costs and benefits of trade are unfairly distributed by governments of the Global North, and the income gap between the rich countries of the Global North and the poor countries of the Global South widens as much as possible. Therefore, today, areas such as global income inequality, multinational corporate policies, foreign investments, and lobbying activities stand out as the main subjects of scrutiny in the global political economy (Giray, 2007; Hahnel, 2014; Marques & Utting, 2010).

For the sake of benefiting from foreign investments, countries design their national policies according to the global economy. For this purpose, incentive policies can pass through the countries' parliaments in line with the wishes of foreign investors. However, although such practices are necessary conditions for foreign investors, they have never been sufficient, since foreign investors want to see legal arrangements made together with economic and financial advantages (Öz, 2012). In case of any conflict that may arise, the aim is to solve the problems by means of the international arbitral tribunal, which they can equally represent, rather than the local courts of the country where the investment was made, since national legal rules are generally insufficient in resolving international investment disputes. Therefore, it is necessary to adapt national law to international law. The political economy of arbitration draws attention to this issue, and tries to explain how political economic approaches direct legal regulations as a result of attempts to get a share from global capital.

The obvious increase observed in international capital flows encourages the arbitration mechanism, not only in the resolution of investment disputes, but also in the solution of the double taxation problem arising from investments, since in practice, unilateral and multilateral double tax avoidance agreements may be insufficient in solving tax problems. On this point, the mutual agreement procedure (MAP) that has come to the fore may contain inadequacies in practice. Therefore, in today's world, where economic activities have become more complex, disputes do not only consist of investment disputes such as electronic commerce, transfer pricing, disguised capital, profit transfer, and investment-related problems. At the same time, it is necessary to assess the negativities arising from the global tax problems and offer suggestions for the solution of these problems. In line with this need, it is understood that in addition to the international commercial arbitration mechanism, the concept of international taxational arbitration mechanism has also been raised. However, discussions over whether the regulations regarding the arbitration mechanism may limit the sovereign power of the countries continue to exist and to be current as one of the main problematics in today's political economy.

2. Definition, History, and Scope of International Arbitration

Arbitration is the resolution of a dispute that may arise on the issues agreed upon by both parties by applying to the arbitrator's decision, outside of the judicial system of a state. In other words, it is an alternative dispute resolution method that allows third parties to resolve a dispute with the consent of all parties (Wild, 2006). It involves the resolution of any dispute issue in accordance with the arbitration agreement or arbitration clause, through persons agreed upon by the parties. It can also be seen as the elimination of a current or future legal dispute through the arbitrator under the arbitration agreement (Collin, 2004; Martin & Law, 2013).

Historically, it is possible to find numerous examples showing the rich history of binding arbitration decisions in ancient Phoenicia in 700 BC, in China 2000 years ago, in India 2500 years ago, and in Ancient Egypt.

Arbitration in ancient Greece: It is seen that self-policing or self-control systems were created through the arbitrator or arbitration mechanism instead of the judge. For Aristotle and Cicero, arbitration was a positive mechanism, a quality that also can be said to define today's arbitration mechanism. Aristotle states that in the arbitration mechanism, the arbitrator can decide in a more egalitarian and fair way than the judge can, since he does not have to apply the rules of law alone. Cicero, then, says that a person who goes to court will face one of two alternatives: winning or losing. A person who goes to arbitration, though, may have the possibility of winning at least to some extent, rather than getting everything. **Arbitration in Roman Law:** In ancient Rome, disputes that arose could be resolved by the arbitration rules under the supervision of third parties, as well as by the judges. In practice, actions against the enforcement of arbitral decisions were met by penal sanctions. After Christianity was accepted as the official state religion in the Roman Empire, church priests were also able to settle some disputes as arbitrators. **Arbitration in Islamic Law:** The application of the method of arbitration for the resolution of various disputes was, from the first days of Islam, a sovereign matter. Thus, local laws were amended to include arbitration. Arbitration law was adopted as part of the basic legal system and arbitrator decisions were also considered to be proportionate to religious provisions. **Arbitration in Medieval Practices:** In the Middle Ages, which came after the fall of the Roman Empire, arbitration emerged as a set of general rules, rather than an exceptional practice, for resolving disputes between nobles. It is also observed that the practice of arbitration was used as an alternative dispute resolution mechanism to the king's court in medieval law. Arbitration essentially constituted a nonviolent process. In the early period, it is seen that even criminal cases were handled by the arbitration procedure. In the following period, it is understood that criminal sanctions against the rights and freedoms of individuals were not subject to arbitration proceedings. **Arbitration in European Commercial Law:** In the 10th and 11th centuries, commercial arbitration was a widely used mechanism in many European cities, under the name of commercial law. The structure in question was founded on legitimacy, justice, mutual benefit, and understanding. Those who refused to enforce an arbitrator's decision during this period also faced exclusion from other traders. The arbitration mechanism continued to operate throughout the process. The fact that the first arbitration law enacted by Ireland in 1698 remained unchanged for 250 years is also proof of the continuity of this process (Barrett & Barrett, 2004; Martin & Law, 2013; Wild, 2006).

The modern roots of the international arbitration mechanism are based on the Jay Treaty (1784) between the USA and the United Kingdom, according to which arbitration commissions were established to resolve legal disputes between states. It is understood that the Hague Peace Conference of 1899 and 1907 also included "peace-oriented" arbitration legislation. As of today, arbitration law is an integral part of customary international law. It is constantly evolving and growing in response to social and economic globalization (Martin & Law, 2013). Parallel to the increase in international commercial relations, the aim is to resolve disputes according to arbitration rules. Thus, problems can be solved at a speed equal to that of globalization (Collin, 2004; Schill, 2014).

The arbitration mechanism is generally applied to commercial disputes. However, many areas – sports, family, inheritance law, industrial and intellectual property rights, etc. – can also benefit from the arbitration procedure. To achieve this, though, the arbitration legislation in the domestic legal systems of the states must be adapted to the international arbitration legislation. Bilateral or multilateral international agreements signed and put into effect between countries form the legal infrastructure of international arbitration.

With the international commercial arbitration mechanism, the foreign investor undertakes to fulfill the public service investments required by the state within the scope of the concession agreement. In case of disagreement, it aims to resolve the problem through international arbitration or arbitration committees, instead of through local judicial bodies. For this purpose, first of all, the parties should include an arbitration clause in the main contract regarding the resolution of all disputes arising from the contract through arbitration. They can then conclude a separate arbitration agreement, and resolve disputes under the arbitration clauses. In practice, there are various types of arbitration. Compulsory arbitration aims to resolve mutual disputes between the parties only through arbitration law, in line with the parties' request, and ultimately to establish an arbitration decision. Non-compulsory arbitration is considered as only one of the resolution methods included in the contract for the settlement of disputes between the parties. Binding arbitration is based on the parties' prior agreement, and clarifies that the arbitration decision taken during the arbitration process must be fulfilled without the right to object or litigate. According to non-binding arbitration, though, the parties do not have an obligation to implement the arbitration decision. In this method, arbitral decisions can be referred to the courts when necessary, as when the arbitrator's decision is appealed. However, the main arbitration method preferred in practice is the mandatory and binding arbitration mechanism (Barrett & Barrett, 2004; Wild, 2006).

The most important concept in the arbitration procedure is the public service concession agreements. Public service concession contracts are contracts that transfer the establishment or operation of public services to a private person. Concession, in administrative law, is only one of the methods that ensure the execution of public services. If the public services are performed by private legal persons under a long-term concession agreement, such as an administrative contract, with their own capital, profit, loss, and damage, this is also called a concession. Governments sometimes resort to this method when infrastructure is lacking, and undertake public services – highways, bridges, dams, energy systems, operation of natural resources, etc. – through private initiatives. In this process, the attempt is often made to resolve disputes arising from investments as a political-economic problem through the international arbitration mechanism, and the arbitration procedure is put in place.

After the parties have agreed to take the dispute to arbitration, the decision must be made whether the abitration will take the form of an institutional arbitration or an ad hoc arbitration unaffiliated with any institution. Both options have advantages and disadvantages. In the institutional arbitration mechanism, the institution – such as the ICC and the ICSID – has effective and established rules that have been tested over time and have been created to deal with many problems that may arise; a decision can be made in relatively a short time. In addition, fees and expenses are paid in advance, and arbitrators are determined and appointed within a reasonable time. However, it is more costly.

In ad hoc arbitration, there is no institution that administers the arbitration, as in institutional arbitration. The parties govern arbitration according to their own rules or prefer to use the UNCITRAL Arbitration Rules in disputes of a temporary nature for special purposes, such as craft. Contemporary provisions for ad hoc arbitration have been published by the United Nations Commission on International Trade Law (UNCITRAL).

However, the point that should be kept in mind here is that the UNCITRAL Arbitration Rules do not constitute an arbitration institution established to administer the arbitration itself, like ICC or ICSID, but are rather only rules for arbitration. Through these rules, the parties or authorized special arbitrators solve the problem. In addition, in ad hoc arbitration, the costs are low and the procedures for the arbitrator and the arbitration process are more flexible, due to the absence of an institution administering the arbitration. On the other hand, this is the main disadvantage of ad hoc arbitration, considering that one of the parties may intentionally disrupt the process due to the swaying of the rules in practice (Collin, 2004; Moses, 2017; Rovine, 2016).

3. The Formation Process of the International Arbitration Mechanism

Developments in the last century have been important in the protection of foreign investments and investors and in the resolution of emerging disputes. In this context, customary law, bilateral and multilateral international agreements, and legal regulations have shaped international arbitration law. In this way, disputes between the investor state and the country where the investment is made can be resolved. However, the attempts of investors to seek their rights through the arbitration mechanism is not a new concept. It is also known that until fairly recently, investment disputes were resolved with an approach based on capitulations and diplomatic protectionism. In fact, it is extremely important at this point that the concept of diplomatic protectionism includes the element of arbitration (Paparinskis, 2008; Rovine, 2016).

Capitulation means surrender agreement. It is a treaty that creates a special and partially unilateral obligation, and refers to the privileges granted by one country to other countries. In this method, external jurisdiction is partially accepted in the resolution of the disputes that arise. In this way, foreign nationals are allowed to be tried in accordance with their own country's laws through diplomatic or consular courts. Through capitulations, foreign investors are taken under protection outside their country. It is possible to find the heaviest form of capitulations in history in the case of the Ottoman Empire. During the Ottoman period, the wide-ranging tax exemptions granted to foreign investors were extremely important. Especially under the term *bac*, transit tax and taxes on exported goods were reduced significantly. This made commercial activities extremely profitable for foreign traders. Colin Imber points out that the tax exemption between Muslim and non-Muslim taxpayers is perhaps the most important determinant of legal status. With the caputulation agreements, foreigners had the opportunity to be tried in their own consulates, in accordance with their own laws, in other disputes apart from taxation issues (Boogert, 2020; Martin & Law, 2013; Schill, 2014).

Another important issue to protect foreign investors is the concept of diplomatic protectionism. Diplomatic protection is the protection provided by the state to its nationals outside of its borders. It allows countries to politicize their investment disputes to the extent that they might even lead to military intervention. However, the arbitration mechanism dissevers investment disputes from claims of diplomatic protection, and allows for the peaceful resolution of problems. It has been observed that foreign investments, especially in Latin American countries, have been subject to diplomatic protectionism since the 1800s. It is understood that military intervention has been used as a legitimate method in the resolution of investment disputes. It is a fact that this process continued until after the Second World War, which is the post-colonial period. Latin American countries have also developed opposition theories against such practices. The most important of these are the Calvo and Drago Doctrines. Both doctrines later had important effects on the policies of other developing regions. The Calvo Doctrine aims to resolve disputes arising from foreign investments under the sovereignty of states by local judicial bodies under all circumstances. Thus, the parties accept from the outset that they will take the problems that arise to the local jurisdiction, by including in the contract a Calvo Condition. In this way, the trial takes place within the geographical boundaries of the state where the investment takes place, based on national law and an understanding that accepts the jurisdiction of national courts. Similarly, the Drago Doctrine – named because it expresses the views put forward by Argentine Foreign Minister Louis M. Drago in 1907 – asserts that the lands of the debtor country cannot be occupied by the states of the creditor country for the purpose of collecting public debts. Another view that emerged within the scope of diplomatic protectionism is the Porter Doctrine, according to which a country that cannot collect its receivables will not immediately be able to use force against the debtor country. Instead, the debtor country will accept the resolution of the dispute by arbitration through the arbitration mechanism. Arbitration decisions are final, and in case of opposition to this decision, resorting to armed force will become legitimate. Therefore, the Porter Agreement is the first multilateral agreement to include a mandatory arbitration clause. In disputes, the parties that declare that the Porter Contractual Provisions will take effect go to arbitration, which is considered primarily a modern approach in the event of a dispute. However, it is clear that the convention approves the use of force in interstate relations (Asouzu, 2004; Bratspies & Miller, 2009; Schill, 2014).

It is a fact that regulations within the scope of capitulations and diplomatic protectionism pose a threat to the integrity of the invested country. This situation has also caused serious concerns from the perspective of developing countries towards foreign investments. Therefore, it has come to the fore that investment disputes are settled through local judicial bodies in the process. The idea of public interest is decisive at this point. Countries have long resisted revising their legal systems on the grounds of public interest. However, this resistance is incompatible with the efforts of developing countries to attract capital, since foreign investors do not want to go to the local judicial body in case of a dispute in order to guarantee the return of capital. In the face of this dilemma, the domestic law boards that represent the interests of the countries do not coincide with the rules of international law. Bilateral and multilateral agreements signed between countries for the elimination of negativities may be insufficient at this point. The international arbitration law that emerged to fulfill this need is a standard practice that allows the parties to meet on common ground.

4. International Legal Regulations on Arbitration

4.1. International Conventions

International conventions are customary rules that have general principles within the framework of international relations, which, once adopted, make international commercial transactions uniform. They can be defined according to geographical, political, economic, legal, or commercial criteria (Noussia, 2010). Along with national laws, international conventions constitute the primary source of power in an arbitration agreement (Onyema, 2010). The main international conventions that govern the application of arbitration are:

- **(i)** The Geneva Protocol (1923): This was the first regulation based on arbitration in international commercial matters (Gaillard & Savage, 1999).
- **(ii)** The Geneva Convention (1927): Signed in 1927 after the Geneva Protocol, it is the Convention on the Recognition and Enforcement of Foreign Arbitrator's Decisions. Its aim is to ensure that the decisions taken in the party countries will be binding on other contracting states to some extent (Moses, 2017).

(iii) The New York Convention (1958): This is the most important international convention in this field. The New York Convention of 1958 regulates how foreign arbitrator decisions are implemented. With this agreement, the reasons for the parties' refusal to recognize the arbitrator decisions are limited and reduced to only a few articles – for example, the violation of public policy or public order. The ability to apply referee decisions was expanded, and the finality of referee decisions was emphasized. The 1923 Geneva Protocol and the 1927 Geneva Convention were abolished with the New York Convention of 1958 (Hornle, 2009; Onyema, 2010).

(iv) European Convention on International Commercial Arbitration (ECICA 1961): The European Convention explains that the cancellation decisions taken for the foreign arbitrator decision are related only to a limited number of issues which are listed (Ambrumenil et al., 1997; Rovine, 2016).

(v) The Washington Convention (1965): This is a contract aimed at resolving investment disputes between states and citizens of other states. It was created under the auspices of the World Bank. The Washington Convention established the International Centre for Settlement of Investment Disputes (ICSID), an institutional arbitration mechanism that specifically handles investment disputes. It offers guarantees for an impartial and efficient resolution of disputes between investors and host countries. Referee decisions are binding. (Gaillard & Savage, 1999; Hornle, 2009).

(vi) The Panama Convention (1975): As a sign of distrust of the New York Convention, Latin American countries signed the Panama Convention in Panama on 30 January 1975. The Panama Convention operates under the umbrella of the Organization of American States (OAS). Fifteen Latin American countries – Argentina, Brazil, Chile, Colombia, Costa Rica, Ecuador, El Salvador, Guatemala, Honduras, Mexico, Panama, Paraguay, Peru, Uruguay, Venezuela, and the United States have been parties to the contract since 1990 (Gaillard & Savage, 1999; Lutz, 1995).

(vii) Agreement on the Mutual Protection and Promotion of Investments (AMPPI): This aims to encourage and protect investments between foreign investors and host states in the regional and sectoral spheres. The agreement includes the arbitration mechanism (Onyema, 2010; Schill, 2014).

(viii) The OECD Multilateral Agreement on Investment (MAI 1998): This has the same characteristics as international investment agreements of a similar nature. However, the agreement is mostly aimed at protecting the interests of developed countries. Therefore, it is signed at a limited level (Schill, 2014).

(ix) The Multilateral Investment Guarantee Agency (MIGA 1985): This agreement aims to resolve disputes between member states through an arbitration mechanism. With this agreement, foreign investors are also protected against political risks, such as expropriation (Asouzu, 2004; Gaillard & Savage, 1999).

4.2. International Arbitration Institutions

Arbitration has emerged as a product of the parties' attempts to seek alternative right, both nationally and internationally. Since its inception, it has made its weight felt in both domestic and international law. However, it is not possible to say that the arbitration institution has a well-established structure; rather, as a part of the new world order, it continues to develop its own institutions and rules through international agreements and conventions. Arbitration has thus become an integral part of international law and the justice system. Because, it is not possible to solve the problems arising from the conflict of different legal systems only with national legal rules in a global world. Therefore, arbitration rules associated with the United Nations Commission on International Trade Law (UNCITRAL) and arbitration institutions such as ICC and ICSID have been established to specifically manage arbitration. There are in fact a number of arbitration institutions operating in this field, such as the American Arbitration Association, the London International Arbitration Court, and other international arbitration institutions.

International Chamber of Commerce Arbitration *(ICC)*

The ICC International Court of Arbitration, operating out of Paris, is the world's best known and the most prestigious arbitration institution. The Arbitration Court has a governing body responsible for overseeing the arbitration process, along with a permanent secretariat made up of professional administrative staff. First of all, in order to apply for arbitral resolution, an arbitration agreement must be made in writing between the parties, and the desire to resolve the dispute through the ICC arbitration committee must be clearly stated. Subsequently, the subjects of dispute, the parties to the dispute, information about the place of arbitration, information on the applicable law, and other information such as the language to be used and the number of arbitral tribunals, must be sent to the ICC. Trials are expected to be completed in about six months. Arbitration decisions taken as a result of the trial are binding and final for the parties. If the parties wish, they can apply to the arbitral tribunal for correction of the decision (Moses, 2017; Schill, 2014).

International Centre for Settlement of Investment Disputes *(ICSID)*

ICSID aims to resolve investment disputes between the state and citizens of other states within the scope of arbitration. Parties that accept arbitration under the ICSID institution are deemed to have waived from resolving the dispute in the rules they will determine. Therefore, the parties are obliged to implement the provisions of ICSID. Bilateral investment treaties also contain provisions regarding the possibility of resorting to ICSID arbitration in case of disagreement. However, the most important feature of ICSID arbitration is that the parties accept the arbitrator's decisions regarding monetary payments as a decision made by the courts of their own countries and immediately fulfill their requirements. It is clear, then, that the arbitrator's decisions are binding and final (Moses, 2017).

The United Nations Commission on International Trade Law *(UNCITRAL)*

Another method aims to resolve conflicts in accordance with the rules prepared by the United Nations Commission on International Trade Law (UNCITRAL). Arbitration rules were established by UNCITRAL in 1976 to be used in international trade. These universally acceptable rules govern arbitration under an ad hoc private arbitration system. In other words, disputes are resolved only under certain rules, not under a certain institution. In this type of arbitration, there is no institution that provides secretarial services, and the arbitration body is formed only for a specific problem, temporarily or incidentally. The parties are obliged to abide by the UNCITRAL rules, but they are also free to use any of these rules. Looking at the content of the rules, we see that they are a reflection of different national rules. Provisions that are found to be useful by experts in international practice are added to the existing rules, and the rules are updated. Thus, the Model Law on International Commercial Arbitration was established in 1985. UNCITRAL arbitrator decisions are binding and final. In addition, the rules are flexible and confidentiality is at the forefront. Company secrets are specifically protected. The Model Law is preferred for reasons such its equal treatment of the parties and being less costly than institutional arbitration (Gaillard & Savage, 1999; Hornle, 2009; Noussia, 2010).

American Arbitration Association *(AAA)*

This is a center established for the resolution of international disputes. Through its offices operating in countries such as Dublin, Ireland, Mexico City, and Singapore, it has provided resolution of investment disputes through arbitration institutions in at least 43 countries. Arbitrator decisions are final and binding (Moses, 2017).

London Court of International Arbitration *(LCIA)*

Established in the late 19th century, this is the oldest international arbitration institution. It is an organization that aims to resolve disputes as quickly as possible. It is a respected arbitration institution that guarantees the supervision of arbitration, the determination of arbitrator problems, the appointment of arbitrators, the control of costs, and the effective functioning of arbitration rules (Moses, 2017).

Other Arbitration Institutions

Other institutions of international arbitration and mediation include the Arbitration Institute of the Stockholm Chamber of Commerce (SCC), the China International Economic and Trade Arbitration Commission (CIETAC), and the World Intellectual Property Organization (WIPO). It is also possible to encounter some special types of arbitration in practice. For example, there are rules and procedures established for the resolution of industrial-based disputes, such as by the Grain and Feed Trade Association (GAFTA), the London Maritime Arbitration Association (LMAA), and the London Metal Exchange (LME) (Hornle, 2009; Moses, 2017).

5. Alternative Resolution Methods and International Arbitration

Globalization has certain effects on cultural, political, and economic life. Such effects manifest themselves not only in the national arena, but also in the international arena. As a matter of fact, one of the transformative processes of globalization is its innovations in international law. The change and transformation observed in tax law, especially in addition to international investment law, has brought the concept of alternative dispute resolution (ADR) to the fore. These are alternative resolution methods that aim to resolve existing disputes outside the courts. In other words, ADR is an umbrella term for mechanisms that allow dispute resolution out of court. As seen in Figure 14, there are bargaining and adjudication methods at both ends of the spectrum in resolving disputes. Although the state judiciary – that is, the litigation mechanism – is included in the current law, the problems are basically resolved by other forms of this structure, such as mediation, arbitration, and negotiation methods. In particular, the use of these methods was frequently advocated by economic-political approaches in the 1970s and 1980s. The main reason for the increasing use of ADR is that it emerged as a response to the shortcomings of the court system, parallel to the development of globalization (Gaillard & Savage, 1999; Hornle, 2009).

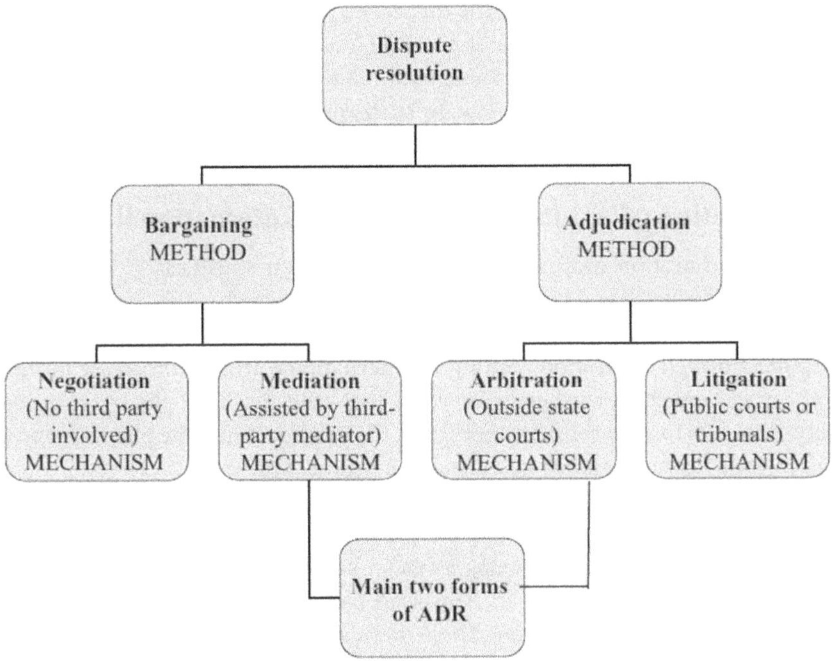

Figure 14: The basic methods and mechanisms of alternative dispute resolution (ADR)
Source: Hornle, 2009

The most basic form of ADR is the negotiation process. The peculiarity of this process is that existing problems between two people or different groups are only negotiated and discussed between the parties, and thus the problem is resolved simply in a way that is acceptable to both parties. In the mediation method, unlike negotiation, an impartial third person is involved in the resolution process. It is sometimes, of course, necessary to make a decision to resolve disputes through arbitration or litigation. However, the mediation method is used when there is no need for such a decision, relying only on the good-willed efforts of the person, called the mediator, who brings the parties together to resolve existing problems (Barrett & Barrett, 2004). In the arbitration method, on the other hand, in order for the dispute to be resolved according to the arbitration rules and the arbitral decision, both parties must agree. Also, while judges are responsible for enforcing the law, arbitrators tend to take recourse to concessions, not just the law. This means that the arbitrator also benefits from natural law rules such as customary rules (Bealey & Johnson, 1999; Martin & Law, 2013). This understanding is also important in terms of revealing the difference between legality and lawfulness, which has existed from the time of ancient Greece to the present. This is due to the fact that court decisions on some issues may be in accordance with legality, but not in accordance with the law. In such cases, resolving existing problems with an arbitrator's decision allows justice to function more soundly.

6. Evaluation of Arbitration in Terms of International Tax Law

With the arbitration mechanism, problems between "businesses", between "a business and a state", and between "states" can be resolved.

In business-to-business arbitration, companies can simply resolve existing disputes through arbitration, putting an international arbitration clause in their contracts. A mechanism thereby emerges that costs less than the court procedure, dissolves in a short time, allows both the defendant and the plaintiff to win, and in which conditions can be extended when necessary.

In the business-to-state arbitration mechanism, the arbitration clause in the agreements between businesses and states is handled. For example, in the case of the Mexican government imposing a tax on beverages with high fructose corn syrup exported to Mexico by an American company, the disputed matter was left to the arbitration institution. The American company ADM filed a lawsuit against the Mexican government on the grounds that discriminatory taxation was applied to them. The Mexican government, however, argued that the tax was legitimate and declared that this situation had a negative impact on sugarcane exports, which constitute its most important export item. It was also pointed out that this situation adversely affected the market expansion activities of the Mexican government. The NAFTA arbitration panel, however, decided that the tax was discriminatory. In 2006, it ruled against Mexico in favor of the American company ADM, which was entitled to 33.5 million dollars in compensation pursuant to this decision (Publiccitizen, 2011).

The most obvious example that can be given for state-to-state arbitration is that of Turkey. The Customs Union Agreement between Turkey and the EU entered into force on 1 January 1996. According to this agreement, Turkey imposed a quantity restriction on textile goods imported from some third countries as per the Common Customs Tariff (CCT) of the European Union. The Indian government, however, objected that such restrictions imposed by Turkey were contrary to the provisions of the GATT/WTO on the removal of discriminatory practices in trade. They argued that Turkey's inclusion in the Customs Union would not constitute a cause for discriminatory restrictions, reasoning that although Turkey entered the Customs Union, it was still not a member of the EU. For this reason, India applied to the ICSID international arbitration committee. With the decision taken on 31 May 1999, the ICSID arbitral tribunal concluded that the restrictions imposed by Turkey on textile and clothing products in 19 categories are contrary to the provisions of GATT/WTO. Turkey's objections were rejected and it was decided that it should fulfill its obligations as soon as possible within the scope of the WTO provisions. Turkey was warned that if its violation of the provisions of the agreement continued, the necessary sanctions and trade bans would be put into effect (World Trade Organization, 1999). Thereupon, although Turkey was reluctant at the beginning, it was compelled to fulfill the requirements of the arbitration decision without shirking its responsibilities.

As can be seen, arbitration is a method mostly used in the settlement of commercial disputes. However, countries may resort to the international arbitration mechanism in all matters requiring reconciliation, including tax dispute issues. For this reason, arbitration is seen as a part of global law that allows effective resolution of existing problems in parallel with the speed of globalization.

The growing role of globalization has led to significant developments since the 1980s. Prominent among these developments are:

- The significant opening up of economies
- The extraordinary growth of international trade
- The increasingly integrated structure of the world economy
- The removal of obstacles to capital mobility
- The extraordinary increase in cross-border capital movements
- The increasing fluidity of direct and indirect (portfolio) investments
- The elimination of current account imbalances
- The provision of the necessary foreign currency for international travel
- The growing power of multinational companies in world trade
- High growth rates in per capita income globally
- The increasing tendency of individuals to spend their increasing earnings abroad

While all these developments have created opportunities for countries, they have also led to negative effects in terms of the tax systems of countries. For this reason, tax authorities have increasingly faced a new generation of problems, and tax problems arising from interstate double taxation have come to the fore (Tanzi, 2007).

The Double Tax Avoidance Agreement (DTAA) is the first method that comes to mind as a means to eliminate existing problems. However, in practice, the desired solution cannot be achieved in cases where the clear rules in the double taxation agreements are misinterpreted or ignored by the tax administrations of the countries. In such cases, problems are generally referred to the Mutual Agreement Procedure (MAP) Article 25 of the OECD Model Tax Convention. As for the inadequacy of this method, just as in the commercial arbitration mechanism, the taxational arbitration mechanism is presented as one of the weighted solution methods.

7. History and Definition of International Tax Disputes

The purpose of the formation of tax agreements is the resolution of tax disputes. The main problems arising in this area relate to the integration of national and international tax laws, at the basis of which is the dilemma that countries face in transferring their tax sovereignty to a higher authority. Especially since the second half of the 19th century, when income tax became increasingly widespread, this issue has been even more evident. Today, the obvious increase in the cross-border relations of countries necessitates potential cooperation in the field of taxation. The rules created by countries taking into account their own national interests are insufficient on this point. For this reason, countries create (i) unilateral, (ii) bilateral, and (iii) multilateral agreements in solving tax problems. Among these, bilateral agreements are extremely important in solving problems. In this way, double taxation can be prevented and international trade can be liberalized. The first bilateral double taxation agreement was prepared on the basis of the German double taxation avoidance law of 1870, and took into account direct taxes. This agreement between Prussia and Austria-Hungary is dated 1899. There were very few similar bilateral tax treaties before the First World War. Although several bilateral tax treaties were concluded after the First World War, basic work on this issue was initiated by the League of Nations in the mid-1920s.

The first model double taxation treaty was made in 1928. In the agreement, a schedular approach was established by making the types of income clear and obvious. However, the League of Nations model did not become very popular, and only twenty bilateral tax treaties emerged from it. After the Second World War, work continued toward the development of two different models within the scope of the United Nations and of the Organization for European Economic Cooperation (OEEC) in the 1950s. OEEC took the name OECD in 1961, and published the first sample tax treaty in 1963. This model, revised in 1977, is extremely important. As of this date, there have been 179 bilateral double tax treaties between OECD member countries. Since 1992, the changes in the OECD Model Convention have been revised and updated every few years. The OECD Model Convention represents the position of developed countries. The

United Nations Model, which follows the OECD Model, includes tax agreements between developed and developing countries – for example, the G20. Although the UN model in the 1980s was updated in 2001, it is largely similar to the OECD Model. As of today, more than 2,500 double taxation agreements are in effect worldwide (Harris & Oliver, 2010; Tanzi, 2007).

A conflict between one country's legislation and the laws of another country is known as a conflict of laws – a term used primarily in the United States and Canada, though it has also come into use in the United Kingdom (Garner, 2019). International commercial disputes are even more significant, given the increasing size of global trade. This situation causes serious problems in the taxation of income and earnings resulting from economic activities. Such problems – referred to as an international tax conflict – constitute the negative results of the intersection of the complex level of the taxational provisions of different countries (Ault & Bradford, 1990; Collin, 2004). Countries, though, apply the right to taxation based on three different principles: source, residence, and nationality. If the countries are willing to use this right to the fullest, tax problems can grow even more. For example, the United States exercises its taxation power on the basis of nationality, taxing its citizens on all income they earn worldwide. The issue of double taxation arises as income is taxed twice, both inside and outside the US (Head, 2007). Although the principle of residence in taxation is a universally accepted principle, its application can vary considerably according to time, place, and situation. Therefore, due to the fact that countries have different perspectives and legal approaches on tax issues, tax disputes continue to be a global problem. As a result of taxing income on taxpayers in more than one country, it presents the problem of international double taxation in economic or legal terms (Ault & Bradford, 1990; Larkins, 2004).

International double taxation refers to the situation in which two or more states tax the same taxpayer on the same income during the same taxation period. This is the narrow legal definition of international double taxation. In economic terms, double taxation is the taxation of the same income over two or more taxpayers. In short, in the legal sense of double taxation, one person is taxed twice on the same income, while in economic double taxation, more than one person is taxed on the same income. The concept of person here refers to either natural or legal persons – i.e., companies. For example, if the dividend of a company based in Turkey, deriving from its investment in the shares of a company based in the United States, is taxed in both the United States and Turkey, a double tax problem occurs in legal terms. On the other hand, the problem of double taxation occurs economically in the taxation of the dividends of a company based in Turkey from its subsidiary operating in the United States.

In the first case, a single person has to pay double tax on the same income, while in the second case, more than one person has to pay tax on the same income (Öz, 2005). In such cases, the problem of international tax dispute arises. Double taxation was, when seen historically, a domestic tax problem in the 19th century; examples would include the collection of property taxes at both the state and local level, or the double taxation of those with property on routes close to both railway and telegraph lines. However, today, the problem of double taxation has become an international problem in parallel with the development of modernity and multinational companies (Ault & Bradford, 1990; Banks, 2010).

In this case, countries can unilaterally solve the double taxation problem by methods such as exception, deduction, or credit. Or, as mentioned above, they can solve problems effectively, mainly through bilateral tax treaties, such as double taxation avoidance treaties (Andersson et al., 2007; Ault & Bradford, 1990). Tax treaties are basically expected to fulfill four functions. They firstly aim to make the taxation regime unified and standardized; towards this end, they try to prevent more than one tax on the same income by limiting the taxation powers between the contracting countries. Secondly, problems arising from transfer pricing are eliminated and tax avoidance methods are reduced. Thirdly, information exchange in taxation is encouraged, and information fluidity increases; in this way, it may be possible to prevent treaty shopping. And fourthly, with the network of bilateral tax treaties, countries are also enabled to make tax reforms (Harris & Oliver, 2010; Neumayer, 2009; OECD, 2010a).

However, despite the explanations above, double taxation problems may arise due to different interpretations of the provisions of the agreement, or to a conflict of authority between the country of origin and that of residence. In the presence of such situations, tax agreements are insufficient, and alternative solution methods may be sought.

8. Resolution of International Tax Disputes

Tax agreements signed between countries have priority in solving problems related to taxation. However, tax agreements are not always effective in solving tax problems. Therefore, it is understood that two basic solution mechanisms have been developed as a result of the intensive efforts of the OECD (Teather, 2005). The first of these is the mutual agreement procedure – in the form of either corresponding adjustments procedure or advance pricing arrangement – which is regulated under Article 25 of the OECD Model Tax Agreement. The second method is the application that allows tax arbitration with the provisions added to the 5th paragraph of Article 25 on the point of the inadequacy of the Mutual Agreement Procedure. Another method other than the OECD is the arbitration practice introduced within the scope of the European Union Arbitration Agreement (Harris & Oliver, 2010). However, in today's world where taxational problems have become more complex, it is seen that taxational arbitration practices, known as alternative solution mechanisms, are strongly recommended by the OECD as a more effective means of engagement. It is in this way that tax disputes caused by double taxation can be most effectively resolved. Among the many problems relating to double taxation, the most important are those arising from transfer pricing. This is because even though disputes are between countries, companies may have to pay taxes on the same income in more than one country. For this reason, while making investment decisions, businesses have to take into account the global tax problems arising from taxational uncertainties, as well as market risk (Andersson, 2020; OECD, 2010b).

8.1. Mutual Agreement Procedure

For the resolution of international disputes arising due to double taxation, recourse is often made to the mutual agreement procedure (MAP), which was established by Article 25 of the OECD Model Tax Convention. With this procedure, double taxation arising from transfer pricing adjustments can be prevented (OECD, 2017; TP Guidelines, 2021).

According to Article 25 of the Model Agreement:

(i). Where a person considers that the actions of one or both of the Contracting States result or will result for him in taxation not in accordance with the provisions of this Convention, he may, irrespective of the remedies provided by the domestic law of those States, present his case to the competent authority of either Contracting State. The case must be presented within three years from the first notification of the action resulting in taxation not in accordance with the provisions of the Convention.

(ii). The competent authority shall endeavour, if the objection appears to it to be justified and if it is not itself able to arrive at a satisfactory solution, to resolve the case by mutual agreement with the competent authority of the other Contracting State.

(iii). The competent authorities of the Contracting States shall endeavour to resolve by mutual agreement any difficulties or doubts arising as to the interpretation or application of the Convention.

(iv). The competent authorities of the Contracting States may communicate with each other directly, including through a joint commission consisting of themselves or their representatives, for the purpose of reaching an agreement in the sense of the preceding paragraphs.

(v). b) the competent authorities are unable to reach an agreement to resolve that case pursuant to paragraph 2 within two years from the date when all the information required by the competent authorities in order to address the case has been provided to both competent authorities, any unresolved issues arising from the case shall be submitted to arbitration if the person so requests in writing. These unresolved issues shall not, however, be submitted to arbitration if a decision on these issues has already been rendered by a court or administrative tribunal of either State (OECD, 2017).

Article 25 of the OECD Model Tax Agreement, or, in other words, the mutual agreement procedure, is the negotiation process between the competent authorities of the countries party to the agreement, aiming to resolve tax disputes effectively and in good faith. Regarding the disputes in question, there may be problems arising from legal or economic double taxation in the form of undue taxation of taxpayers, as well as inconsistencies arising from the implementation and interpretation of a contract. In such cases, the taxpayer forwards the illegal taxation to the competent authority of the country of residence or of citizenship, and may request that the problem be resolved between the parties in agreement with the mutual agreement procedure. Historically, most of these cases were economic double taxation issues arising from the taxation of intra-group transactions by one or more tax administrations on multinational companies, within the scope of transfer pricing. In addition, the most important feature of MAP is that if the problems cannot be resolved within two years according to mutual agreement, the parties can go to arbitration (Avi-Yonah, 2007; Deutsch et al., 2008; Harris & Oliver, 2010).

However, the mutual agreement procedure may contain inadequacies due to the following reasons: (i) Although the taxpayer has the right to request the mutual agreement procedure, the initiation of the process is entirely at the discretion of the competent authorities; (ii) Enforcement of decisions taken in the MAP process may involve uncertainties; (iii) Taxpayers do not have the right to obtain information about the trial process or the case – MAP is generally maintained by the competent authorities of the contracting states; (iv) The major shortcoming of MAP is that the competent authorities do not have an obligation to ultimately reach a decision – in other words, there is no obligation to make a final decision on the elimination of double taxation; and (v) There is no obligation to publish the concluded agreements, which prevents precedent decision-making (Altman, 2005).

In practice, the mutual agreement procedure takes one of two forms: corresponding adjustments approach, and advance pricing agreements.

a) Corresponding Adjustments Approach

The corresponding adjustments approach is considered a form of the mutual agreement procedure in practice. The aim is to eliminate the double taxation problem arising from transfer pricing. The counter-adjustment approach is regulated in article 9 of the OECD Model Tax Agreement, under the title of associated enterprises (OECD, 2010b). The text states:

(i). Where

a) an enterprise of a Contracting State participates directly or indirectly in the management, control or capital of an enterprise of the other Contracting State,

or

b) the same persons participate directly or indirectly in the management, control or capital of an enterprise of a Contracting State and an enterprise of the other Contracting State, and in either case conditions are made or imposed between the two enterprises in their commercial or financial relations which differ from those which would be made between independent enterprises, then any profits which would, but for those conditions, have accrued to one of the enterprises, but, by reason of those conditions, have not so accrued, may be included in the profits of that enterprise and taxed accordingly.

(ii). Where a Contracting State includes in the profits of an enterprise of that State and taxes accordingly profits on which an enterprise of the other Contracting State has been charged to tax in that other State and the profits so included are profits which would have accrued to the enterprise of the first-mentioned State if the conditions made between the two enterprises had been those which would have been made between independent enterprises, then that other State shall make an appropriate adjustment to the amount of the tax charged therein on those profits (OECD, 2008b; OECD, 2017).

b) Advance Pricing Arrangement

Today, the increase in electronic commerce, the spread of the internet, the ease of communication and transportation, the easy availability of goods and services, and the spread of transfer transactions all over the world are the hallmarks of economic globalization. Advance pricing agreements, which emerged as an American innovation in parallel with these developments, are one of the regulations that take into account the increasing trends in trade. The OECD, in its report of October 1999, published the arrangements for advance pricing agreements based on the mutual agreement procedure, in consideration of the fact that they can be useful in areas where traditional transfer pricing related mechanisms have failed (Avi-Yonah 2007; OECD, 2010a; OECD, 2010b).

Advance pricing arrangement (APA) is an arrangement that predetermines the content of controlled transactions. Controlled transactions describe the criteria used to determine the transfer price for transactions to be carried out for a certain period in advance. These criteria include the analysis of method, data, adjustments, and critical assumptions about future events. Advance pricing arrangements can be made unilaterally between a tax administration and a taxpayer, or multilaterally in the form of an agreement among two or more tax administrations (OECD, 2017). These agreements are used to determine the transfer price between a multinational company and related parties. In the determination of the price to be used, the administration and the taxpayer agree on the predetermined criteria and make price adjustments. These agreements also allow taxpayers to make tax planning. The process of the agreement begins with the application of taxpayers. While unilateral advance price agreements are not often made, bilateral advance price agreements are quite common (Harris & Oliver, 2010; OECD, 2017).

This method provides for prior agreement between the competent authorities and taxpayers on transfer pricing principles for a certain period of time, in order to avoid double taxation. It provides convenience in cross-border transactions for a certain period without being non-arm's length to the parties. By asking for an advance pricing arrangement in cross-border transactions, a taxpayer not only significantly reduces the possibility of double taxation, but also more effectively prevents the problems arising from taxation between the tax authorities and the taxpayer. This method thus aims to resolve disputes between taxpayers and governments with a proactive approach by taking precautions beforehand. In addition, this plays an active role in reducing costs (OECD, 2007; OECD, 2017).

For example, in the USA, advance pricing agreements are signed between the Internal Revenue Service (IRS) and companies, thus saving the parties from other costs such as litigation, loss of time, and uncertainties. To date, more than 150 APAs have been signed between parties. Many of these arrangements are multilateral agreements signed between the IRS and different multinational companies. Similarly, upfront price agreements have been signed between Australia and the United States on the basis of the Reciprocal Agreement Procedure. At the request of taxpayers in Australia or the USA, the competent authorities of each country consult with each other. In this way, transfer price adjustments are made to prevent taxpayers from being subjected to double taxation on income tax, deductions, and payments made (Avi-Yonah, 2007; Deutsch et al., 2008).

In advance pricing agreements, the competent authorities of the countries party to the agreement participate in the process. In cases that are not clearly stated in the APA, the attempt is made to solve the problems by mutual agreement method according to Article 25 of the OECD Model Tax Convention. The most important advantage of APA is to increase predictability in tax matters arising from international transactions. Thus, the uncertainty in the sharing of the global tax base is eliminated, certainty in tax transactions is ensured, and a favorable tax environment for investment is established. When the APA expires, it can be extended again. It also creates an opportunity for consultation and mutual cooperation between tax administrations and taxpayers on complex tax issues. The free flow of information is encouraged, costly and time-consuming practices are prevented, and prolonging situations such as litigation are prevented (OECD, 2017).

However, in practice, advance pricing arrangements can also cause significant tax problems for both tax administrations and taxpayers. In particular, unilateral advance price arrangements may be insufficient in solving the economic or legal double taxation problem of multinational companies (MNCs) compared to bilateral or multilateral APAs. Investigations or excessive penalties may also arise under the agreement. In addition, since the private information of the taxpayers can be requested easily, there may be concerns that the trade secrets of the parties cannot be protected during the examinations. Again, while some tax administrations exhibit a very cooperative attitude, some tax administrations may not exhibit the same behavior. Similarly, authorities can make advance price agreements on artificial methods and conditions in the calculation of effective prices, or an unsuccessful definition of the tax base may occur through tax-oriented transactions. Considering these and similar negativities, recommendations that taxational arbitration procedure should be included within the scope of tax agreements often come to the fore (OECD, 2010a; OECD, 2010b; Teather, 2005).

8.2. Tax Arbitration Practices in the OECD and the EU

In international trade relations, bilateral and multilateral agreements – especially double taxation agreements – play an important role in resolving international disputes. They even play a constitutional role in the global economy (Schill,

2014). However, the problems arising from the implementation of double taxation agreements lead to the continuation of tax problems in the international arena. In this case, trying to solve the problems with the mutual agreement procedure – whether corresponding adjustments or advance pricing arrangement – is one of the most frequently used methods. However, these methods have disadvantages as well as advantages, and consequently it is not always possible to achieved the desired results. To address such deficiencies, recourse to taxational arbitration practices within the scope of the OECD and the EU is widespread around the world.

While disputes arising from international investments bring the commercial arbitration mechanism to the agenda, tax problems arising from international double taxation also bring taxational arbitration practices to the fore. Taxational arbitration provisions have been included in bilateral and multilateral tax agreements since 1989. The tax agreement signed between the USA and Germany in 1989 is the first bilateral tax agreement in force that includes an arbitration provision. In this respect, it also constitutes the infrastructure of taxational arbitration law (Altman, 2005).

The taxational arbitration mechanism is one of the current practices that is frequently recommended by international committees for the resolution of tax disputes. Arbitration is in demand because it guarantees the legal rights of investors in accordance with international standards, prevents discriminatory treatment, protects property rights, ensures fair and equal treatment, and emerges as an impartial method in dispute matters. In addition, the arbitration mechanism allows for the protection of investor rights more effectively in independent arbitral decisions. In this process, disputes can be resolved through institutional arbitration, depending on an institution, or it can be resolved on an ad hoc basis without being affiliated with an institution. This situation allows the parties to solve their problems by means of any rule or institution they wish. In addition, arbitration provides the parties with the opportunity to evaluate the costs and risks of the conflict in advance, increases the legal predictability, and provides the opportunity for foreign investors to exit at the point where local courts cannot be impartial (Asouzu, 2004; Gottschalk et al., 2007; ICLG, 2019).

The arbitration procedure is essentially carried out as either a binding (compulsory) or a non-binding (voluntary) arbitration process. The main difference between compulsory arbitration and voluntary arbitration is that in voluntary arbitration, the parties can apply to the courts when necessary. Therefore, although there is credibility for voluntary arbitration, the emphasis is on compulsory arbitration. The binding arbitration procedure (BAP) is included in the process as an extension of the mutual agreement procedure (MAP) and occurs in two different types. The first is the arbitration procedure for commercial profit and transfer pricing only in certain matters, as included in the double tax avoidance agreements between the USA and Germany and between the USA and Canada. The second type of binding arbitration is included in the double tax avoidance agreements between the USA and Belgium, and covers all matters that fall within the jurisdiction of the competent authorities (Deutsch et al., 2008; Hornle, 2009). However, in cases in which the agreement within the scope of MAP is not binding, the attempt is made to resolve problems with the non-binding arbitration method, relying on expert opinion (Avi-Yonah, 2007; Moses, 2017).

a) Arbitration Practices Within the Scope of the OECD

Countries are establishing increasingly comprehensive procedures and institutions for the resolution of disputes arising from international trade and investments. On the basis of resolution mechanisms, there are arbitration institutions and arbitration rules composed of independent persons. It is understood that arbitration was brought to the agenda of OECD member countries for the first time in relation to the problems encountered in the transfer pricing process. The OECD recommends using the arbitration mechanism in resolving disputes. Article 25 of the OECD Model Tax Agreement, published in 1977, defines the arbitration institution as an expert opinion in the form of independent arbitrators who can be consulted. In the report published in 1984, there are discussions on making more use of the arbitration procedure in order to maintain the relations between countries in a consistent manner and to prevent the problem of double taxation. As a result, it was decided that it would not be appropriate to advise the parties on the arbitration process, since in the mentioned period, the arbitration agreement was still in draft form. Procedures for resolving disputes are still immature. In addition, the arbitration procedure has not yet entered into bilateral tax treaties. Transfer price disputes were not as intense as they are today. Therefore, for these and similar reasons, whether the taxational arbitration process is a suitable solution method for international tax problems continues to be debated (ICLG, 2019; OECD, 2017).

In the following period, investments gained an international dimension and trade increased significantly, causing tax disputes to take on an international character. In other words, such disputes no longer occur only between the taxpayer and the tax administration to which he is affiliated, but in the form of various disputes between the tax administrations of different countries (OECD, 2010b). Thereupon, on 27 July 2004, the OECD Financial Affairs Committee published a progress report on the settlement of cross-border tax disputes. The original name of the report was "Improving the Process for Resolving International Tax Disputes." This report consists of 31 proposals to avoid double taxation. Then, on 30 January 2007, the Financial Affairs Committee accepted the report on the use of arbitration practices in the resolution of tax disputes, and the report was published by the OECD in February 2007 (OECD, 2007).

At this point, problems related to double taxation can be resolved with MAP. However, MAP is not a guaranteed solution in cases where negotiations between tax administrations do not yield results. For this reason, with the fifth paragraph added to the 25th article of the OECD Model Tax Agreement in 2008, it is recommended to solve the problems with the arbitration method, and this approach emerges as an extension of the MAP (OECD, 2010b).

When a person is faced with taxation that does not comply with the provisions of the treaty due to the actions of one or both of the contracting states, he submits the problem to the competent authority of one of the contracting states. The competent authority also expects the problem to be resolved within two years from the date on which it conveyed the problem to the competent authority of the other contracting state. For unresolved issues, though, arbitration can be made upon the request of the taxpayer. However, if there is already a decision given by the courts in any of the contracting states regarding the unresolved issues, then arbitration will not be possible. If the issue is still in court and has not been resolved, arbitration can still be applied. The established arbitration decision is binding on both contracting states. The arbitral decision will be implemented and enforced immediately, regardless of the statute of limitations in the domestic legislation of the states (OECD, 2008b).

b) Arbitration Practices Within the Scope of the European Union

European Union law puts new practices into effect for solving international tax problems that arise within the Union. This is even more important considering the increasing number of members (Harris & Oliver, 2010). To guarantee the free movement of people, goods, and capital within the EU requires the prevention of the double taxation problem arising from international tax problems (Deutsch et al., 2008; Teather, 2005). In this context, many commission reports have been published in order to eliminate the tax barriers arising from the cross-border commercial activities of companies within the EU. As a result of these efforts, the convention titled "On the elimination of double taxation in connection with the adjustment of profits of associated enterprises," or the EU Arbitration Convention, came into effect in 1990. The Arbitration Convention aims to reduce the risk of double taxation that may occur in intra-Union enterprises.

With the arbitration agreement, the EU Commission aims for:

- The elimination of barriers arising from the existence of very different national tax systems,
- A reduction in the risk of double taxation arising from transfer pricing disputes,
- The prevention of uncertainties in the tax field, and
- The elimination of the inadequacies of national tax administrations.

The Transfer Pricing Agreement, or Arbitration Agreement, which was signed by the member states of the European Union in 1990 and entered into force on 1 January 1995, is accepted and used as one of the most important resolution methods in resolving tax disputes (Cerioni, 2007; OECD, 2017).

The provisions introduced under the Arbitration Agreement are essentially regulations aimed at eliminating the double taxation risk for profit transfer and transfer pricing. In this context, the expert group formed by the European Commission in 2002 and consisting of member state representatives started its work under the name EU Joint Transfer Pricing Forum. The expert group focuses on the improvements that can be made to avoid double taxation and the practical suggestions that can be made in this regard. As a result of these studies, two Codes of Conduct have emerged. The first code of conduct, published in 2004, aims to ensure the effective and uniform application of the 1990 Arbitration Convention by member states. The second code of conduct proposed in 2005 consists of the regulations that standardize the documents used by multinational companies in cross-border transactions. The EU arbitration process, which emerged as a result of these developments, also appears as a binding, mandatory arbitration process (Cerioni, 2007; Cerioni, 2015).

The arbitration provisions in the EU Arbitration Convention are based on or are similar to the arbitration provisions in paragraph (5) of article 25 of the OECD Model Tax Convention. Therefore, it is possible to say that the OECD has a direct impact on the EU Arbitration Convention. On this point, the most important issue of distinction is that the EU Arbitration Convention is supported by the Code of Conduct. However, the EU Arbitration Convention is narrower in scope than the arbitration procedure in the OECD Model Tax Convention, since it only applies to disputes regarding transfer pricing and profit distribution between headquarters and associated companies. In the operation of the process, first of all, the taxpayer requests the prevention of double taxation within the scope of the Arbitration Convention by applying to the authorized administration of the contracting state of which he is a citizen or in which he is residing. If the problem cannot be resolved, the relevant administration requests the settlement of the dispute by applying to the other administration. However, in accordance with Article 7 of the Arbitration Convention, competitive authorities are established if an agreement cannot be reached within two years from the date the question was first presented. The Commission expresses its opinion within a maximum of six months from the date the question is referred to it, and makes decisions by absolute majority. Competent authorities, such as tax administrations, should make a decision to eliminate double taxation within the next six months, based on the opinion of the commission, and reach an agreement between them. Otherwise, the commission opinion comes into play and the parties become bound by the commission opinion on the elimination of double taxation. The EU Arbitration Agreement is thus a mandatory contract, and at the same time encourages states to resolve their problems through mutual agreement. It is also noted that the European Court of Justice can be assigned for tax disputes (Harris & Oliver, 2010).

Arbitration is a special form of judgment that aims to resolve international disputes through an impartial third party – namely, the arbitrator – a process in which the decisions made are binding and compelling (Hornle, 2009). Today, the General Agreement on Tariffs and Trade (GATT), the World Trade Organization (WTO), the International Monetary Fund (IMF), and institutions such as the North American Free Trade Agreement (NAFTA) also support the arbitration mechanism in resolving existing disputes (OECD, 2017). In addition, the International Chamber of Commerce (ICC) draws attention to the necessity of an arbitration mechanism, in addition to methods such as consultation, cooperation, and reconciliation, for the resolution of cross-border commercial disputes. Especially in international disputes, international investors put forward the arbitration clause as a precondition for their investments, since local courts may exhibit biased attitudes (Gottschalk et al., 2007; Schutter, 2010).

On the other hand, international arbitration is often met with backlash in developing countries. They say that subjecting developing countries, which are at different stages of economic development, to the same law as societies in the developed world will lead to inequality from the start. They argue that the practice of arbitration is a product of the political extensions of the developed countries and the practical manifestation of the colonial order that the European states defended in their favor in the past. In addition, the concerns about the impartiality and independence of the arbitrators, as well as the reservations that the arbitrators may act in their own interests, are among the most frequently expressed criticisms (Asouzu, 2004; Brower & Schill, 2010). Another criticism brought against international arbitration is that developed countries can take the initiative in the formation of arbitration commissions. On the other hand, the lack of qualified personnel to manage the process in this area is another concern. In addition, the arbitrators may be biased in determining the law to be applied to the subject of the dispute. In some cases, compensation amounts and litigation expenses can be costly. The most important matter of concern is related to the issues arising from the fact that developing countries that have to open up to the outside world due to economic integration are, in accepting such practices, transferring their independence to a supranational authority (Asouzu, 2004; Brower & Schill, 2010; Onyema, 2010).

Despite all these negative views on international arbitration, the use of the arbitration mechanism has not decreased over time; on the contrary, it is increasing. Arbitration is one of the most widely used methods in the resolution of tax disputes, as well as in the resolution of investment disputes. At this point, although it is a private legal system – lex arbitri – it has become institutionalized as a subsystem in accordance with international law. It has produced consistent and uniform decisions in the decision-making process with arbitration courts (Moses, 2017; Onyema, 2010; Schill, 2014). In this process, arbitration courts can easily conduct research and access necessary evidence. The national laws of countries, however, do not impose any restrictions on the use of these powers, since international conventions oblige their application (ICLG. 2019; Schill, 2014).

As a result, in the case of tax disputes, taxpayers can first apply to the local courts in the country where the dispute is in question or request the resolution of the problems with MAP. However, at the point of the inadequacy of the MAP, arbitration can be made upon the request of the taxpayer and if the relevant countries' tax administrations agree on the arbitration clause. For this purpose, it is obligatory for the relevant administrations to agree on a draft agreement that includes the arbitration clause for the resolution of disputes (OECD, 2017). However, it is likely that the taxational arbitration mechanism will be one of the main analytical methods in the future, just like the commercial arbitration mechanism. In fact, considering the extent that international economic activities have reached, it is almost essential to develop global law.

General Evaluation and Conclusion

Political economy analysis (PEA) aims to situate development interventions within an understanding of the prevailing political and economic processes in society – specifically, the incentives, relationships, distribution, and contestation of power between different groups and individuals. In other words, political economy defines the mutual interaction of politics and economy (Mcloughlin, 2014). In general, economics shows how unlimited human needs can be met efficiently with limited resources. According to this definition, the concept of economy is discussed from a general point of view through the problem of scarcity and choice. As such, the starting point of political economy focuses on "how politics affects economic choices," as well as "the political structure of the decision-making process" (Sezgin, 2005).

Political economy is a normative area of study. Economics, on the other hand, strives to be independent of value judgments. The attempt was made to transform political economy into a branch of science such as mathematics and physics under the influence of Marshall. After the publication of Paul Samuelson's book *Foundations of Economic Analysis* in 1947, complex mathematical models came to dominate the study of economy. Thus, while political economy became two separate disciplines such as politics and economy, the process of separation of political economy was completed. Political economy has also turned into a field of science called economics. However, what we call international political economy is the whole of approaches that deal with international economy and international relations together. In other words, it is a field of science that explains the processes of globalizing capitalism and the complex politics and power struggles that emerge from it (Jackson et al., 2019).

As Ostrovitianon stated, it is extremely important to make visible and understand political economy through class approaches – bourgeois, petty bourgeois, and proletariat – in order to understand capitalism. Similarly, the aim of Marxist political economy is to try to lay down the laws of economic development, so that by making use of these laws, the workers will defeat capitalism and ensure the political and economic transformation of society. The unique interests of the working class will also feed the process of social development. Therefore, it is essential to understand the coexistence of politics and economy in order to stand against the capitalist regime, to end the exploitation of man by man, to prevent the division of society into classes, and to ensure that society is redesigned (Ibarrola, 1987).

When we consider them as a political philosophy, today's neoliberal policies tend to protect a handful of private interests, maximize financial investments, and control social life through legal regulations. At the center of neoliberal philosophy is the understanding that everything should be left to the functioning of the market, and this is extended to cover a wide area from the regulation of markets to the regulation of law. This situation is perceived as a handicap even within democracies, and it is understood that analyses that fail to take into account the effects of politics on the economy will constitute nothing more than subjective approaches (Scott, 2009).

References

Ackerman, J. (2002). Food: How altered? *National Geographic Magazine*. https://www. nationalgeographic.com/environment/global-warming/food-how-altered/. Access: 22 May 2018.

Agrawal, R., & Pinilla, F.G. (2012). Metabolic syndrome in the brain: Deficiency in omega-3 fatty acid exacerbates dysfunctions in ınsulin receptor signalling and cognition. *The Journal of Physiology*, 590(10), 2485–2499. DOI: 10.1113/jphysiol.2012.230078.

Allen, F., & Gale, D. (2004). Financial intermediaries and markets. *Econometrica*, 72(4), 1023–1061. DOI: 10.1111/J.1468-0262.2004.00525.X.

Altman, D. (2005). *Dispute resolution under tax treaties*. International Bureau of Fiscal Documentation. IBFD Publications.

Ambrumenil, F.P., Scott, W., & Ambrumenil, L. (1997). *Meditation & arbitration for lawyers*. Cavendish Publishing Limited.

Andersson, E. (2020). *Reconstructing the global political economy: An analytical guide*. Bristol University Press.

Andersson, K., Eberhartinger, E., & Oxelheim, L. (2007). The role of national tax policies in the European Union. in: K. Andersson., E. Eberhartinger., & L. Oxelheim (eds.), *National tax policyin Europe*. Springer-Verlag, Berlin, Heidelberg.

Ardebili, E.Y. (2015). Investigation of the effects of consumption high corn fructose syrup on maternal and fetus of rats ruring gestation. *Post Graduate Thesis*, Hacettepe University. http://www.openaccess.hacettepe.edu.tr:8080/xmlui/bitstream/handle/11655/2021/6a06721c-d716-4592-8a87-50fb5ba02d8b.pdf?sequence=1

Art, R.J., & Jervis, R. (1985). *International politics: Anarchy, force, political economy, and decision making*. Little, Brown and Co.

Asouzu, A. (2004). *International commercial arbitration and African States: Practice, participation and institutional development*. Cambridge University Press.

Ault, H., & Bradford, D. (1990). Taxation in the global economy. *National Bureau of Economic Research Project Report*. The University of Chicago Press.

Avi-Yonah, R. (2007). *International tax as international law: An analysis of the international tax regime*. Cambridge University Press.

Bache, I., Bulmer, S., George, S., & Parker, O. (2014). *Politics in the European ünion*. Oxford University Press.

Baker, V., Gvakharia, M., Rone, H., Manalad, J., & Adamson. D. (2008). Economic cost forimplementation of the U.S. food & drug administration's code of federal regulations. *American Society for Reproductive Medicine*, 90(3), 537–545. DOI: 10.1016/j. fertnstert.2007.06.100

Balaam, D.N., & Veseth, M. (2004). *Introduction to international political economy*. Taylor & Francis.

Baldwin, R., & Winters, L.A. (2004). *Challenges to globalization: Analyzing the economics*. The University of Chicago Press.

Banks, E. (2010). *Dictionary of finance, investment and banking*. Palgrave Macmillan.

Barrett, J.T., & Barrett, J.P. (2004). *A History of alternative dispute resolution*. Jossey-Bass.

Barry, R., Angelo, L., Buzzanell, P., & Gray, F. (1990). *Sugar: background for 1990 farm legislation*. Economic Research Service. https://www.ers.usda.gov/webdocs/publications/41833/50510_ages9006.pdf?v=0

Bauman, Z. (1998). *Globalization: The human consequences*. Columbia University Press.

Bealey, F., & Johnson, A. (1999). *The blackwell dictionary of political science*. Blackwell Publishing Ltd.

Beams, N. (2018). *Marx's analysis of the laws of capital and the share market crisis*. Boston. https://www.wsws.org/en/articles/2018/02/17/marx-f17.html

BeMiller, J., & Whistler, R. (2009). *Starch: Chemistry and technology*. Macmillan Publishing.

Bennett, R.M. (2010). *Food fights: International regimes and the politics of agricultural trade disputes*. Routledge.

Bernholz, P., & Vaubel, R. (2007). *Political competition and economic requlation*. Routledge.

Bishop, M. (2004). *Essential economics*. Profile Books Limited.

Bocarsly, M.E., Powell, E.S., Avena, N.M., & Hoebel, B.G. (2010). High-fructose Corn syrup causes characteristics of obesity in rats: Increased body weight, body fat and triglyceride levels. *Pharmacol Biochem Behavior*, 97(1), 101–106. DOI:10.1016/j.pbb.2010.02.012

Boccara, N. (2010). *Modeling complex systems*. Springer.

Bocock, R. (1993). *Consumption*. Routledge.

Bodley, J. (2013). *The Small nation solution: How the world's smallest nations can solve the world's biggest problems*. Lanham, MD: AltaMira Press.

Boogert, M.H. (2020). *The capitulations and the ottoman legal system: Qadis, consuls and beratlls in the 18th century*. Brill Academic Pub.

Bracking, S. (2009). *Money and power: Great predators in the political economy of development*. Pluto Press.

Braithwaite, J., & Drahos, P. (2000). *Global business regulation*. Cambridge University Press.

Bratspies, R.M., & Miller, R.A. (2009). *Transboundary harm in international Law*. Cambridge University Press.

Brennan, G., & Buchanan, J.M. (2000). *The Power to tax: Analytical foundations of a fiscal Constitution*. Cambridge University Press.

Brower, C., & Schill, S. (2010). Regulating counsel conduct before international arbitral tribunals. in: P. Bekker., R. Dolzer., & M. Waibel (eds.), *Making transnational law work in the global economy*. Cambridge University Press.

Brown, A.C. (2019). *Understanding food: Principles and preparation*. Boston, MA: Cengage Learning.

Bulut, Y. (2017). SBS: starch-based sugar and cancer. *Star Gazetesi*. http://www.star.com.tr/yazar/nbs-nisasta-bazli-seker. Access:12 Aug 2017.

Bundschuh, J. (2012). *Sustainable energy developments*. CRC Press.

Burstein, P., & Linton, A. (2002). The impact of political parties, interest groups, and social movement organizations on public policy. *Social Forces*, 81(2), 380–408. DOI:10.1353/sof.2003.0004

BWI (Bread for the World Institute). (2007). Healthy food, farms & families: Hunger 2007. *17th Annual Report on The State of World Hunger*.

Carrion, G. (2010). Business, politics and free trade negotiations in Nicaragua: Who were the winners and losers? in: J.C. Marques., & P. Utting (eds.), *Business, politics and public policy: Implications for inclusive development*. Palgrave Macmillan.

CDC (Center for Disease Control and Prevention). (2017). *Chronic disease prevention and health promotion*. Department of Health & Human Services, Atlanta-U.S. https://www.cdc.gov/chronicdisease/index.htm. Access: 26 Nov 2017.

Cerioni, L. (2007). *EU corporate law and EU company tax law*. Edward Elgar.

Cerioni, L. (2015). *The European Union and direct taxation*. Routledge.

CFI (Corporate Finance Institute). (2021). *Political economy*. CFI Education Inc Press.

CFTC (The Commodity Futures Trading commission). (2018). *Reauthorization. agriculture, nutrition, forestry*. https://www. agriculture. senate. gov/issues/cftc. Access: 05 Jan 2018.

Chamlee-Wright, E. (2010). Beyond the status quo, in the world and in the discipline. in: R. Garnett., E. Olsen., & M. Starr (eds.), *Economic pluralism*. Routledge.

Collin, P.H. (2004). *Dictionary of law*. Bloomsbury Publishing Plc.

Congleton, R., & Hillman, A. (2015). *Companion to the political economy of rent seeking*. Edward Elgar Publishing, Cheltenham.

Dalal, A.K. (2000). Living with a chronic disease: Healing and psychological adjustment in indian society. *Psychology and Developing Societies*, 12(1), 68–81. DOI:10.1177/097133360001200105.

Dalgalıdere, S. (2011). An overview of critical political economy. *DÜ. İİBF Dergisi*, 1(2), 70–85.

Das, D.K. (2006). Globalization in the word of finance: An analytical history. *Global Economy Journol*, 6(1), 1–25.

Davis, C., & Abraham, J. (2013). *Unhealthy pharmaceutical regulation: Innovation, Politics and promissory science*. Palgrave Macmillan. ISBN: 978-0-230-00866-3

Debroy. D. (2004). *Dictionary of economics*. Sterling Publishers.

Demirgüç, K., & Detragiache, E. (2002). Does deposit insurance increase banking system stability? An empirical investigation. *Journal of Monetary Economics*, 49(1), 1373–1406. DOI: 10.1016/S0304-3932(02)00171-X

Deutsch, R.L., Arkwright, R., & Chiew, D. (2008). *Principles and practice of double taxation agreements: A question and answer approach*. BNA International Inc.

Dinar, G., & Somel, C. (2017). Economic surplus in Turkey. *ODTÜ Gelişme Dergisi*, 44(8), 155–176.

Dittmann, R. (2012). *Brighton Baby a revolutionary organic approach to having an extraordinary child*. Balboa Press.

Draycott, P. (2007). *Sugar beet*. Blackwell Publishing Ltd.

Drazen, A. (2001). *Political economy in macroeconomics*. Princeton University Press.

Dreher, A., Gaston, N., & Martens, P. (2008). *Measuring globalisation: Gauging its consequences*. Springer.

Eğilmez, M. (2015). *Siyasal ekonomi ve davranışsal ekonomi*. http://www.mahfiegilmez.com/2015/11/siyasal-ekonomi-ve-davranssal-ekonomi.html

Enderwick, P. (2006). *Globalization and labor*. Chelsea House Publishers.

Erk, O. (2017). *Rediscover your health*. Ankara: Nobel Yayınevi.

Erkızan, H.N. (2002). Küreselleşmenin Tarihsel ve Düşünsel Temelleri Üzerine. *Doğu-Batı Dergisi*, 5(18): 57–70.

Esposito, J. (2016). *Prescription for extreme health*. Health Plus Publishing.

EU sugar policy. (2018). *EU-mercosur negotiations round: Crunch time*. http://sugarcane.org/global-policies/policies-in-the. Access: 09 Feb 2018.

European Commission. (2017). The end of the sugar production quotas in the EU. *European Commission press release, 29 september*. Brussels. http://europa.eu/rapid/press-release_MEMO-17-3488. Access: 11 May 2018.

European Parliament. (2017). *Parliamentary questions*. http://www.europarl.europa.eu/sides/. Access:17 Apr 2018.

Fahey, D. (2017). *Cost and consequences of chronic disease management*. OpenPresentation, National University of Ireland. http://slideplayer.com/slide/2801093/. Access: 19 Oct 2017.

Featherstone, M. (2007). *Consumer culture and postmodernism*. 2th edition. SAGE Publications.

Fromm, E. (2017). *Beyond the chains of illusion: My encounter with Marx and Freud*. Bloomsbury Academic.

Gaillard, E., & Savage, J. (1999). *InternationaI commercial arbitration*. Kluwer Law International.

Garner, B.A. (2019). *Black's law dictionary*. 11th Edition, Thomson Reuters.

Garnett, R., Olsen, E.K., & Starr, M. (2010). *Economic pluralism*. Routledge.

Ghodke, N.B. (2002). *Dictionary of economics*. Atlantic Publications.

Gilpin, J.M. (2001). *Global political economy: Understandıng the internatıonal economic order*. Princeton University Press.

Giray, F. (2007). The privatization and liberalization of telecommunications a comparative analysis for Turkish telecommunications sector. *European Journal of Scientific Research*, 17(4), 546–559.

Giray, F. (2016). *Vergi teşvik sistemi ve uygulamaları*. Ekin Yayınevi.

Golding, P., & Murdock, G. (1991). Culture, communication and political economy. in: J. Curran., & M. Gurevitch (eds), *Mass media and society*. Edward Arnold.

Gottschalk, E., Michaels, R., Ruhl, G., Hein, J.V. (2007). *Conflict of laws in a globalized world*. Cambridge University Press.

Grossmann, M. (2012). Interest group influence on US policy change: An assessment based on policy history. *Interest Groups & Advocacy*, 1(2), 171–192. DOI: 10.1057/iga.2012.9

Hahnel, R. (2014). *The abc's of political economy*. Pluto Press.

Hahnel, R. (2010). From competition and greed to equitable cooperation: What does a pluralist economics have to offer? in: R. Garnett, E.K. Olsen, M. Starr (eds.), *Economic Pluralism*. Routledge.

Harris, B., & Andrew, C. (2011). *Disciplinary and regulatory proceedings*. Jordans.

Harris, P., & Oliver, D. (2010). *International commercial tax*. Cambridge University Press.

Harvey, D. (1985). *The marxian theory of the state*. Wiley.

Head, K. (2007). *Elements of multinational strategy*. Springer-Verlag, Berlin.

HealthData.gov. U.S. (2018). *Department of health & human services*. https://www.healthdata.gov/. Access: 16 Jan 2018.

Herbst, M. (2013). The bank bailout cost US taxpayers nothing? Think again. *The Guardian*, Tue 28 May. https://www.theguardian.com/commentisfree/2013/may/28/bank-bailout-cost-taxpayers. Access: 18 Feb 2018.

Heron, T. (2012). *The global political economy of trade protectionism and liberalization*. Routledge.

Hornle, J. (2009). *Cross-border internet dispute resolution*. Cambridge University Press.

Hui, H., Huang, D., McArthur, D., Nissen, N., Boros, L., & Heaney, A. (2009). Direct spectrophotometric determination of serum fructose in pancreatic cancer patients. *Pancreas*, 38(6), 706–712. DOI: 10.1097/MPA.0b013e3181a7c6

Hyman, M. (2011). *5 reasons high fructose corn syrup will kill you*. Cleveland Clinic Center. http://2011/05/13/5-reasons-high-fructose-corn-syrup-will-kill-you. Access: 27 Dec 2017.

Ibarrola, J. (1987). *Political economy: Alienation and humanism*. Ser publishing

IBISWorld. (2017). High fructose corn syrup production (US): industry report. *Market Research Reports*. https://www.ibisworld.com/industry-trends/specia lizedmarket-research. Access: 18 Mar 2018.

ICLG (International Comparative Legal Guide). (2019). *International arbitration*. Global Legal Group Ltd.

IEG Vantage. (2018). *Sugar & cocoa-agribusiness intelligence*. https://agribusin essintellig ligence.informa.com/products-and-services/data-and-analysis/ieg- vantage/ sugar-cocococoa. Access: 16 Apr 2018.

IMF. (2022a). All economies-reported portfolio investment assets: Total portfolio investment. Coordinated portfolio investment survey (CPIS). data.imf.org/

IMF. (2022b). Rising caseloads, a disrupted recovery, and higher inflation. World Economic Outlook Update.

IronTriangles. (2018). *Study notes*. https://www.tutor2u.net/politics/reference/irontriangles. Access: 08 Mar 2018.

IUORF. (2020). *Political economy: Basic concepts of political economy*. Istanbul University Open and Remote Faculty of Education Publications.

Jackson, R., Moller, J., & Sorensen, G.(2019). *Introduction to international relations theories and approaches*. Oxford University Press.

Jakob, V. (2009). *Discipline in the global economy: International finance and the end of liberalism new political economy*. Taylor & Francis.

Joskow, P., & Noll, R. (1981). Regulation in theory and practice: An overview. in: G. Fromm (ed.), *Studies in public regulation*. Cambridge: The MIT Press.

Jurenas, R. (2004). Sugar policy issues. in: D.L. Sandrino (ed.), *Farm economic issues*. Nova Science Publishers.

Karaca, Y. (2017). SBS sugar or poison? *Yeni Mesaj Gazetesi*. http://www.yenimesaj.com. Access:11 Feb 2018.

Karaoğlu, M. (2011). *High fructose corn syrup*. *Gıda Mühendisliği Dergisi*, 14(33), 1–13.

Kaymakçı, M. (2018). Which sugar is more dangerous? Starch-based sugar. *E-Gazete*. https://www.yenivatan.at/hangi-seker. Access:14 Feb 2018.

Keeney, R.L. (1997). Estimating fatalities ınduced by the economic costs of regulations. *Journal of Risk and Uncertainty*, 14(1), 5–23. org/stable/41760838

Kellner, D. (2002). Theorizing globalization. *Sociological Theory*, 20(3), 285–305.

Keyman, E.F., Sarıbay, A.Y. &Yaşar, A. (1998). Küreselleşme, siyaset ve toplumsal yaşam. İç. E.F. Keyman, A.Y. Sarıbay (der.), *Küreselleşme, sivil toplum ve İslam*. Vadi Yayınları.

KFF (Kaiser Family Foundation). (2012). How much does the U.S. spend on health and how has it changed? *Report*, Word Press. https://www.kff.org/report-section/health-care-costs-a-primer-2012-report/

Kıymaz, T. (2002). *Şeker politikalarında yeni yönelimler ve Türkiye'nin konumu. Yayın no: DPT 2652*. https://www.sbb.gov.tr/wp-content/uploads/2022/07/Seker-Politikalarinda-Yeni-Yonelimler-ve-Turkiyenin-Konumu.pdf

Knoema. (2022).*The portfolio investment of the world*. https://knoema.com/data/portfolio-investment

Kocaman, Ç.B. (2003). *Finansal piyasalar*. Siyasal Kitabevi.

Koch, R. (2014). *The 80/20 principle and 92 other powerful laws of nature: The science of success*. Nicholas Brealey Publishing.

Koç, Y. (2014). Marksist emek değer kuramı ve emperyalist dönemde kapitalist sömürü. *Bilim ve Ütopya Dergisi*, 239. http://yildirimkoc.com.tr › usrfile › 1401701915b

Kohonen, M. (2009). Rationale for world public finance: Mapping the tools for social change. in: M. Kohonen., & F. Mestrum (eds.), *Tax justice: Putting global inequality on the agenda*. Pluto Press.

Korves, R. (2011). *High fructose corn syrup (HFCS) in the U.S. caloric sweetener supply*. Report for the Corn Refiners Association: 1-8. http://www.cornnaturally.com

Kothari, V. (2010). *Executive greed: Examining business failures that contributed to the economic crisis*. Palgrave Macmillan.

Krichner, C. (2007). Public choiice and new instutiotional economics: A comparartive in search of co-opertaion potentials. in: P. Baake., & R. Borck (eds), *Public economics and public choice*. Springer.

Lakhani, H. (1980). Automobile fuel regulations: Direct benefit-cost analysis. *Applied Energy*, 6(4), 301–313. DOI: 10.1016/0306-2619(80)90020-3

Lambsdorff, J.G. (2002). Corruption and rent-seeking. *Public Choice*, 113(1–2), 97–125. DOI: 10.1023/A:1020320327526

Landis, M. (1987). *The politics of chaos*. Susquehanna University Press.

Larkins, E.R. (2004). *International applications of U.S. income tax law*. John Wiley and Sons Inc.

Lee, M. (2002). The effect of sulfur regulations on the U.S. electric power industry: A generalized cost approach. *Energy Economics*, 24(5), 491–508. DOI:10.1016/S0140-9883(02)00011-7

Lust, H.C. (1927). *Abridged reports of the interstate commerce commission and current digest of decisions under the interstate commerce act*. The Traffic Law Book.

Lustig, R. (2013). *Fat chance: Beating the odds against sugar, processed food, obesity, and disease*. Penguin Publishing.

Lutz, D.S. (1995). *The OSCE court of conciliation and arbitration*. Institute for Peace Research and Security Policy at the University of Hamburg.

Lyons, F. (2010). *Fructose exposed: The sweet truth about America's expanding waistline and failing health*. Xulon Press.

Ma, L., Ahmed, E., & Fagan, J. (2014). *High-fructose corn syrup: Health and economic effects*. The State University of New Jersey. DOI: 10.7282/T3G162S6

Mansfield, E.D. (2004). *International conflict and the global economy*. Edward Elgar Pub.

Marques, C., & Utting, P. (2010). *Business, politics and public policy*. International Political Economy Series. Palgrave Macmillan.

Martin, E., & Law, J. (2013). *A dictionary of law*. Oxford University Press.

Marx, K. (1992). *Capital: A critique of political economy-volume III*. 3rd edition. Penguin.

MEP (Marksist Ekonomi Politik). (2020). *Marksist Ekonomi Politik ve İletişim Ders Notları. Ankara Üniversitesi Açık Ders Malzemeleri*. https://acikders.ankara.edu.tr/course/view.php?id=5471

McConnell, M. (2017). *U.S. sugar production*. United States Department of Agriculture, USDA. https://www.ers.usda.gov/publications/pub-details/?pubid=83931

McGivern, G., Fischer, M. (2012). Reactivity and reactions to regulatory transparency in medicine, psychotherapy and counselling. *Social Science & Medicine*, 74(3), 289–296.

Mcloughlin, C. (2014). *Political economy analysis: Topic guide*. UK: GSDRC, University of Birmingham.

Mesquit, E. (2017). *Political economy for public policy*. Princeton University.

Michaud, D., Liu, S., Giovannucci, E., Willett, W., Colditz, G., & Fuchs, C. (2002). Dietary sugar, glycemic load, and pancreatic cancer risk in a prospective study. *Journal of the National Cancer Institute*, 94(17), 1293–1300. PMID: 12208894

Milgate, M., & Stimson, S. (2011). *After Adam Smith: A century of transformation in Politics and political economy*. Princeton University Press.

Milgrom, P., & Roberts, J. (1998). The internal politics of the firm. in: S. Bowles., M. Franzini., & U. Pagano (eds.), *The politics and economics of power*. Taylor & Francis.

Milonakis, D., & Fine, B. (2009). *From political economy to economics: Mill's conciliation, Marx's transgression*. Routledge.

Mishkin, F. (2006). *The next great globalization: How disadvantaged nations can harness their financial systems to get rich*. Princeton University Press.

Mitchell, D. (2005). Sugar policies: An opportunity for change. in: A. Aksoy., & J.C. Beghin (eds.), *Global agricultural trade and developing countries*. Washington, DC.

Mosco, V. (2009). *The political economy of communication*. SAGE Publications.

Moses, M. (2017). *The principles and practice of ınternational commercial arbitration*. Cambridge University Press.

Mueller, D. (2011). The importance of self-interest and public interest in politics. *Critical Review*, 23(3), 321–338. DOI: 10.1080/08913811.2011.635870

Napalkov, N.P. (2009). Prevention and control of non-communicable disease. in. B.P. Mansourian (ed.), *Global perspectives in health*. Eolss Publisher.

Nar, M. (2020). *Kamu ekonomisi: Teori, politika ve uygulama*. 2.baskı. Nobel Yayınevi.

Nar, M. (2021). The relationship between income inequality and energy consumption: A Pareto optimal approach. *Journal of Asian Finance, Economics and Business*, 8(4), 613–624. DOI: 10.13106/jafeb.2021.vol8.no4.0613

Nar, M.Ş. (2015). The effect of globalization on consumption culture: Technology consumption. *The Journal of International Social Research*, 8(37), 941–955. DOI:10.17719/jisr.20153710659

Nar, M., & Nar, M.Ş. (2019). An updated assessment of the OECD's quality of life index. *Problemy Ekorozwoju–Problems oF Sustainable Development*, 4(1), 7–18.

Nar, M., & Nar, M.Ş. (2020). The effects of regulatory authorıtıes on sugar markets: An evaluation of the USA case. *International Journal of Contemporary Economics and Administrative Sciences*, 10(2), 273–299

Neumayer, E. (2009). Do double taxation treaties increase foreign direct investment to developing countries? in: K. Sauvant., & L. Sachs (eds.), *The effect of treaties on foreign direct ınvestment*. Oxford University Press.

Niemi, E. (2003). *The EU sugar regime and forthcoming wto obligations*. Finland: MTT Economic Research.

Noussia, K. (2010). *Confidentiality in ınternational commercial arbitration*. Springer.

Oates, W.E. (2005).Toward a second generation theory of fiscal federalizm. *International Tax and Public Finance*, 12(4), 349–373.

Oatley, T. (2018). *International political economy*. Routledge.

Odabaşı, Y. (2006). *Tüketim kültürü: Yetinen toplumdan tüketen topluma*. Sistem Yayıncılık.

OECD. (1998). *Sugar policy reform: Competition policy issues*. Committee for agriculture.

OECD. (2007). *Manual on effective mutual agreement procedures (MEMAP)*. Centre for Tax Policy and Administration.

OECD. (2008a). *OECD glossary of statıstıcal terms*. OECD publications.

OECD. (2008b). *Model tax convention on income and on capital*. OECD Committee on FiscalAffairs.

OECD. (2010a). *Tax policy studies: Tax policy reform and economic growth*. OECD Publications, no: 20.

OECD. (2010b). *Transfer pricing guidelines for multinational enterprises and tax adminis- trations*. OECD Publications.

OECD. (2011). *Attractiveness for innovation: Location factors for ınternational investment*. OECD Publications.

OECD. (2017). *Transfer pricing guidelines for multinational enterprises and tax adminis- trations.* https://doi.org/10.1787/tpg-2017-en

Onyema, E. (2010). *International commercial arbitration and the arbitrator's contract.* Routledge.

Opalinski, H.A. (2012). High fructose corn syrup, mercury, and autism is there a link? *Journal of the American Academy of Special Education Professionals*, 1(2), 113–129. https://files.eric.ed.gov/fulltext/EJ1135692.pdf

Öz, N. S. (2005). *Uluslararası vergi rekabeti ve vergi cennetleri.* Maliye ve Hukuk Yayınları.

Öz, N. S. (2012). Controlled foreign company regime in Turkey and its valuation. *Intertax*, 40(11), 643–647. DOI: 10.54648/taxi2012066

Öztürk, N. (2020). *Maliye politikası.* Ekin Yayınevi.

PAHO (Pan American Health Organization). (2001). *Investment in health: Social and economic returns.* Scientific and Technical Publication.

Paparinskis, M. (2008). Investment arbitration and the law of countermeasures. *British Yearbook of International Law*, 79(1), 264–352.

Paquin, S. (2019). *International political economy.* SAGE Handbook, Volume III, pp. 1256–1271.

Pawłowski, A. (2009).The sustainable development revolution. *Problemy Ekorozwoju-Problems of Sustaiınable Development*, 4(1), 65–76. https://ekorozwoj.pollub.pl/index.php/number-412009/

Pawłowski, A. (2013). Sustainable development and globalization. *Problemy Ekorozwoju-Problems of Sustainable Development*, 8(2), 5–16. https://ekorozwoj.pollub.pl/index.php/number-822013/

Pelaez, C., & Pelaez, C. (2008). *Globalization and the state: Trade agreements, inequality the environment, financial globalization, international law and vulnerabilities.* Volume II. Palgrave Macmillan.

Peltzman, S. (1976). Toward a more general theory of regulation. *Journal of Law Economics*, 19(2), 211–240. DOI: 10.1086/466865.

Peltzman, S. (1989). The economic theory of regulation after a decade of deregulation. Brookings Papers on Economic Activity: Microeconomics.

Peterson, K. (2018). *Health system tracker.* https://www.healthsystemtracker.org/indicator/spending/health-expenditure-gdp/#Total%20national%20health%20expenditures%20as%20a%20percent%20of%20Gross%20Domestic%20Product,%201970-2020

Pleunie, H. (2017). Sweetness and satiety. in: B. Tepper., & M. Yeomans (eds.), *Flavor, satiety and food intake.* John Wiley & Sons.

Pomeranz, J.L. (2016). *Food law for public health.* Oxford University Press.

Posner, R.A. (1999). *Natural monopoly and its regulation*. Cato Inst.

Publiccitizen. (2011). *Table of foreign ınvestor-state cases and claims under. NAFTA CAFTA and Peru FTA*. https://www.citizen.org/wp-content/uploads/migration/investor-state-chart-april-2011.pdf

Pulszky, Á. (1888). *The theory of law and civil society*. T. Fisher Unwin Publishing.

Ranney, A. (2000). *Governing: An introduction to political science*. Prentice Hall.

Reinsdorf, M., & Slaughter, M. (2009). Challenges in measuring trade in services. in: M. Reinsdorf., & M. Slaughter (eds.), *International trade in services and intantgibles in era of globalization*. The University of Chicago Press.

Richardson, B. (2009). *Sugar: Refined power in a global regime*. Palgrave.

Ritzer, G. (2009). *Enchanting a disenchanted world: Continuity and change in the cathedrals of consumption*. SAGE Publications Inc.

Rovine, A.W. (2016). *Contemporary ıssues in ınternational arbitration and mediation*. Brill.

Rowley, C. (2008). Public choice and constitutional political economy. in: C. Rowley., & F. Schneider (eds.), *Readings in public choice and constitutional political economy*. Springer.

Rudra, N. (2008). *Globalization and the race to the bottom in developing countries: Who really gets hurt?* Cambridge University Press.

Rupert, M., & Solomon, M. (2006).*Globalization and international political economy: The politics of alternative futures*. Owman & Littlefield Publishers.

Schill, S. (2014). *The Multilateralization of international investment law*. Cambridge University Press.

Schmitz, A., & Christian, D. (1993). The economics and politics of U.S sugar policy. in: S.V. Marks., & K.E. Maskus (eds.), *The economics and politics of world sugar policies*. The University of Michigan Press.

Schutter, O. (2010). Sovereignty plus in the era of interdependence. in: P. Bekker., R. Dolzer., & M. Waibel (eds.), *Making Transnational Law Work in the Global Economy*. Cambridge University Press.

Scott, T. (2009). *Dangerous writing: Understanding the political economy of composition*. Utah State University Press.

Segura, J., & Braun, C.R. (2004). *An eponymous dictionary of economics: A guide to laws and theorems named after economists*. Edward Elgar.

Sever, Ç. (2015). The structure, function and transformation of regulatory agencies in Turkey. *AÜHFD*, 64(1), 195–236. DOI: 10.1501/Hukfak_0000001777.

Sezgin, Ş. (2005). Theoretical approaches to politics and economics. *Journal of Management and Economics Research*, 3(4), 133–156.

Singh, J. P. (2010), *International cultural policies and power*. Palgrave Macmillan.

Small, M. (2011). *Dynamics of biological systems*. Chapman and Hall.

Starch-Europe. (2017). *The end of EU sugar production quotas and its impact on sugar consumption in the EU*. https://starch.eu/blog/2017/06/20/starch-europe. Access: 20 June 2018.

Statista. (2018). *Health system: National health expenditure*. The Statistics and Studies Sources. https://www.statista.com/markets/412/topic/454/health-system/#overview

Statista. (2020). *Forecast volume of high fructose corn syrup produced in the European Union (EU 27) from 2015 to 2028*. https://www.statista.com/statistics/549759/high-fructose-corn-syrup-consumption-volume-european-union-28/

Steger, M. (2017). *Globalization: A very short introduction*. Oxford University Press.

Stiegler, B. (2010). *For a new critique of political economy*. Polity press.

Stigler, G.J. (1971). The theory of economic regulation. *The Bell Journal of Economics and Management Science*, 2(1), 3–21. DOI: 10.2307/3003160.

Sugrue T.J., & Maher W.F. (1993). *Globalization of the mass media*. U.S. department of commerce: National telecommunications and information administration.

Tanzi, V. (2007). Fiscal policy in the future: Challenges and opportunities.*CAS Working Paper Series*. Centre for Advanced Studies & New Economics School.

Taubes, G. (2007). *Good calories, bad calories: Challenging the conventional wisdom on diet, weight control, and disease*. Borzoi Book.

Teather, R. (2005). *The benefits of tax competition*. Institute of Economic Affairs.

Thussu, D.K. (2006). *International communication: Continuity and change*. Bloomsbury Academic.

Tomlinson, J. (1999). *Globalization and culture*. University of Chicago Press

TP Guidelines. (2021). *Mutual agreement procedure*. https://tpguidelines.com/

Tubaro, P. (2010). History of economic thought. in: R.C. Free (ed.), *21st century economics: A reference handbook*. SAGE Publications, Inc.

Tullock, G. (1989). *The economics of special privilege and rent seeking*. Kluwer Academic Publishers.

Tullock, G. (2007). Comment: foreign policy and regulation. in: P. Bernholz., & R. Vaubel (eds.), *Political competition and economic requlation*. Routledge.

Tullock, G., Seldon, A., & Brady, G.L. (2002). *Government failure: A primer in public choice*. Cato Institute.

UN. (2018). *Trade, multilateral cooperation and sustainable development*. United Nations Conference on Trade and Development.

UNCTAD. (2020). *World investment report*. United Nations Publication, Geneva.

USDA. (1996). *Agricultural outlook special supplement*. United States Department of Agriculture, Economic Research Service.

USDA. (2018). *Sugar and sweeteners outlook*. United States Department of Agriculture, Economic Research Service.

Valdez, S., & Molyneux, P. (2015). *An introduction to global financial markets*. Palgrave.

Varzakas, T., Labropoulos, A., & Anestis, S. (2012). Syrup. in: T. Varzakas., A. Labropoulos., & S. Anestis (eds.), *Sweeteners: Nutritional aspects, applications, and production technology*. CRC Press.

Veblen, T. (2014). *The theory of the leisure class*. http://moglen.law.columbia.edu/LCS/theoryleisureclass.pdf

Veseth, M., & Balaam, D.N. (2020). *Political economy*. University of Puget Sound Tacoma, Washington. https://www.britannica.com/contributor/Michael-A-Veseth/5696

Viscusi, W., Vernon, J., & Harrington, J. (2005). *Economics of regulation and anti-trust*. The MIT Press.

Vogli, R. D. (2013). Progress or collapse: The crises of market greed. Routledge.

Walter, A., & Sen, G. (2009). *Analyzing the global political economy*. Princeton University.

Walters, S.J.K. (1993). *Enterprise, government and the public*. McGraw-Hill Education.

Wasko, J., Murdock, G., & Sousa, H. (2011), *The political economy of communications: Core concerns and ıssues*. Blackwell Publishing Ltd.

Wellness Tips. (2007). *High fructose corn syrup (glucose-fructose)*. http://www.wellnesstips.ca/high%20fructose%20corn%20syrup.htm. Access:17 Apr 2017.

White, J.S. (2013). Challenging the fructose hypothesis: New perspectives on fructose consumption and metabolism. *Advances in Nutrition*, 4(2), 246–256. DOI: 10.3945/an.112.003137.

White, J.S. (2014). Sucrose, hfcs, and fructose: History, manufacture, composition, applications, and production. in: J.M. Rippe (ed.), *Fructose, high fructose corn syrup, sucrose and health*. Springer.

Wild, S.E. (2006). *Law dictionary*. Wiley Publishing.

Williams, R. (2011). *An introduction to trading in the financial markets: Technology, networks and data*. Elsevier.

Wiltgen, T.J. (2007). An economic history of the United States sugar program. *Thesis*. Montana State University. https://scholarworks.montana.edu/xmlui/bitstream/handle/1/2554/WiltgenT1207.pdf

Winden, F. (2004). Interest group behavior and ınfluence. in: C. Rowley., & F. Schneider (eds.), *The encyclopedia of public choice*. Kluwer Academic Publishers.

Winston, C. (2006). *Government failure versus market failure*. Brookings Institution Press.

World Bank. (2022a). *Portfolio equity, net inflows* (BoP, current US$).

World Bank. (2022b). *Foreign direct investment, net Inflows*. https://data.worldbank.org/indicator/BX.KLT.DINV.CD.WD?most_recent_value_desc=false

World Trade Organization. (1999). Turkey– restrictions on imports of textile and clothing Products. *Report of the Panel*, WT/DS34/R, 31 May 1999.

Yalçın, S. (2017). Açtırma bayramlık ağzımı. *Sözcü*. https://www.sozcu.com.tr/2017/yazarlar/ soner-yalcin/. Access: 11 July 2017.

Yandle, B. (2001). Public choice and the environment. in: W.F. Shughart., & L. Razzolini (eds.), *The Elgar companion to public choice*. Edward Elgar Publishing.

Index

www.ingramcontent.com/pod-product-compliance
Ingram Content Group UK Ltd.
Pitfield, Milton Keynes, MK11 3LW, UK
UKHW021014120926
8556IPUK00040B/1143

9 783631 890677